How To Be

The

SUNDAY SCHOOL TEACHER

They

REMEMBER

How To Be

The

SUNDAY SCHOOL TEACHER

They

REMEMBER

Your Workbook and Planner

Walt Atkins

Covers were designed by Rob McDorman.

Print information available on the last page.

Prior book by Walt Atkins:
How to be the SALESMAN
They Remember (2012)

Rev. date: 12/22/2023

Contents

> [19] *Go therefore and make disciples of all the nations, baptizing them in the name of the Father and of the Son and of the Holy Spirit, 20* **teaching** *them to observe all things that I have commanded you; and lo, I am with you always, even to the end of the age." Amen.—Matthew 28:19-20 (Emphasis added)*

Dedication

Dedication for this book is four-fold. First, to God for His grace, His unmerited favor, upon two young Sunday School teachers, to teach together for over four decades. It extends to Pastor Greg Barkman who offered the opportunity in 1980, and third, to Bruce Councilman who completed the team in 1982. Fourth, dedication extends to over 250 students who have survived our classroom since 2000. Earlier students have sent many sons to us when they reached sixth grade, and some even have grandchildren now. Records before 2000 are unavailable. (Read post card #54.)

We are grateful to the parents who entrusted their sons to us for an important year in their lives. I am personally thankful also to the late George Webb, a man of faith, whom God used to bring our family to Burlington in 1980, to sell for his printing company. One day a customer, a career counselor, confided in me that he wished he knew what success in life was. I told him that I knew. He sat bolt upright. "It's finding God's will for your life and following it." God has blessed us richly all our years.

Meet the Author

Walt Atkins, BS Journalism, Maryland '72, is an author for the second time, having published *How to be the Salesman They Remember* in 2012, following his 31-year career in sales, and retiring in 2010. Now in his fifth decade teaching Sunday School, he writes about the joy that brings.

He worked in the sports information office all during college, served as Assistant Sports Information Director at N.C. State six years, and as SID at East Carolina for two. At all three universities he published numerous award-winning sports media guides. He holds a private pilot's license and served two elected four-year terms on the Graham City Council.

Walt has taught Sunday School at Beacon Baptist Church under Pastor Greg Barkman since 1980. Walt and his wife Pam reside in Graham, NC, have one daughter and four grandchildren. Daughter Cristy Slawson and family served as missionaries in Russia before returning to the USA, now residing in Sioux Falls, SD, where her husband Thomas is an associate pastor.

About the Title

When I first considered this book I wrestled with the title. My first book was titled, *How to be the Salesman They Remember.* After 31 years in sales, I knew it was important that an effective salesman be one that each customer can remember favorably. It was a "How To" book with detailed information and guidance for the aspiring career salesman. I wanted this volume to also be a "How To" book, but my motivation was to encourage teaching of God's Word to energize students to study it for themselves, be converted, live for Jesus, and continue to study the Word. Paul wrote in II Timothy 2:2 that teachers should teach well, to equip students to teach others.

Good students are known to fondly remember their best teachers, the ones who expect, perhaps even demand, the most from them. But I didn't want to project in any way that this Sunday School teacher, or any other Sunday School teacher, was more important than the Word of God. Handling the Word correctly, in a way that it is memorable, is the objective. Nonetheless, I wanted to maintain the "How To" format that would energize a current or prospective teacher to give their very best to teach the class placed in front of them to be enthusiastic about the Word and a lifetime of service to Christ.

So please use this as a guide book to fashion your own teaching methods suitable for the group you have the privilege to teach. For example, students receive a postcard at home each week to let them know what we will study the next Sunday. Maybe a card every month, or occasionally would be more suitable for your class. Can you find a pre-class activity that works best for your group? Greet the class with goals and end the year with students having a confident awareness of what they have learned during the year. In short, plan your year's work and work your plan to achieve the goals you set. Likely your students will be surprised at how much they have learned!

Finally, this is a workbook and a planner written to help you achieve your goals as a Sunday School teacher. We underline in our Bibles to help us find particular passages more easily. Please make use of the ample space and charts provided throughout the text to record your thoughts and plans for Sunday School classes.

So, I kept the title as a "How To" book with the hope that your students will know they had a good teacher, one dedicated to delivering a correct understanding of God's Word, of salvation in the Lord Jesus, and instilling a determination to pursue a lifetime of service to the Lord. *—Walt Atkins*

Preface

When COVID struck America and the world it took many lives and changed many others. It changed society. Schools were closed. Students were denied the face-to-face instruction. It closed many businesses, churches and other institutions, too. Parents became alarmed that their children missed up to two years of fruitful instruction.

Well, the same thing happened to Sunday Schools across America. One of the major casualties that resulted from COVID was that it halted many personal ministries, like hospital, retirement community, and in-home visitation. Worship services continued online with an empty auditorium. We tried online Sunday School for a while, but that proved difficult and was less than satisfactory.

Churches lost Sunday School teachers to the disease itself. Then after a year away, many teachers never returned to their classrooms. New teachers were needed, but lingering effects of social distancing, issues of age, and an abundance of caution caused few newcomers to begin teaching. Across the country more Sunday School teachers are needed. It is my hope that readers can understand, adapt and apply elements from this "How-To" guide book to your specific classroom and its needs. I would urge every committed Christian to accept the opportunity to teach Sunday School. It will enrich your spiritual life, deepen your Bible study, and be a blessing to your students.

Teaching Sunday School is an important responsibility. You will learn so much when you teach. God has given preachers, teachers and other gifts to the Church. Be used of God for His purposes and His glory. This space is usually reserved for the author, but it will finish with some former students telling what Sunday School and their teachers meant to them.—Walt Atkins

Dear Mr. Atkins, Thank you so much for the shirt and taking me to the Carolina game. You have been about my best Sunday School teacher and I am sad that I have to go! Your Student, Ryan

Dear Mr. Atkins, Today we studied I Cor. 12. We learned the importance of every part of the body of Christ functioning as it should. I think of you, because you took time with me. Sincerely, Antonio

Mr. Atkins, Thank you so much for making my 18th birthday a very unique and special surprise. I am very grateful for the men which God has used to influence my life. You have been instruments in the hands of God. I hope Saturday's occasion will serve as a stepping stone as I grow as a man and as a Christian. Your gift will challenge me every time I use or see it. Thanks again for being an important part of my life. Sincerely, Gabe

Dear Mr. Atkins, Thank you for letting me come over last Sunday. I had a lot of fun. I like the Sunday School class. It is fun. Love, Kyle

Dear Walt, I don't know how to properly express my deepest gratitude to you and Pam. I am still overwhelmed that you and your wife would drive all the way to Chicago to see me. I can honestly say I have never seen such generosity of time and effort. Perhaps someday I can possess a fraction of your energy and zeal. Since your visit, both of my supervisors told me how happy they are to have met you. The impression you left helped them see more potential in me as an eager and enthusiastic employee. Thank you again for all you have taught me, both in the classroom and more importantly in the legacy you have left by God's grace. You are teaching me more now than ever about what it means to be a part of the body of Christ. In Christ, David

---

*[11] And He Himself gave some to be apostles, some prophets, some evangelists, and some pastors and **teachers**, [12] for the equipping of the saints for the work of ministry, for the edifying of the body of Christ.—Ephesians 4:11-12 (Emphasis added)*

Forward

By Hunter Strength,
Beacon Youth Pastor

Sunday School holds a dear place in my heart as it has stood as a shining light along the pathway that is my Christian journey. Having sat beneath the ministry of Sunday School teachers for as long as I can remember, it has proven to be an invaluable asset in forming much of my thinking as a believer. This ministry has not only touched my life as a student but has been the means of great blessings as I share in the laborious honor that is found in serving as a teacher.

With this being the case, I find my heart yearning for a new generation of zealous teachers to hold not only the hearts of students, but the word of God with serious commitment. United with the desires of my heart stands the mind of Walt Atkins as he has offered forth a clarion call to studious believers everywhere to pick up the mantle of saints gone by and to commit to serving for the edifying formation of young minds everywhere.

Having served as a Sunday School teacher for over forty years, Walt is experientially qualified to produce this encouraging and practical invitation to the Church. It has been a privilege of mine to witness Walt's vulnerability as he regularly seeks accountability not only in his teaching ministry, but in his devotional life as well. However, the extent of my observation of his ministry has does not end there as I, as the Minister of Youth, am the recipient of the students who have studied under him. In my experience, these students arrive with an impressive familiarity with the thematic concepts of the Scriptures, a patient attentiveness, and an eager sense of preparation that is not the product of mere happenstance. This is the result of a class with teachers sacrificially committed to serious mindedness not only in study, but in cultivating a fruitful atmosphere.

As we observe the inescapable obsession with "self" all around us, there is found a burdensome issue of building the "kingdom of self" from which the Church herself is not immune. Addressing this problem, Walt invites believers to serve in this capacity with a mindfulness toward unity with the pulpit of their individual assemblies as well as the parents of these students. Trailing behind this philosophy is a desire to cultivate a fruitful and repetitious diet of truth to be found in the lives of young minds everywhere. I encourage those who are nervous fence-sitters or hoarders of biblical wisdom to give this a prayerfully read this book with a discerning heart for God's call to this field.

*[1] My brethren, let not many of you become **teachers**, knowing that we shall receive a stricter judgment.—James 3:1 (Emphasis added)*

[58] Therefore, my beloved brethren, be steadfast, immovable, always abounding in the work of the Lord, knowing that your labor is not in vain in the Lord.—I Corinthians 15:58

[105] Your word is a lamp to my feet And a light to my path.—Psalm 119:105

How Our Teaching Started

It is a great responsibility to teach a Sunday School class. If it was easy anyone could do it. But it isn't easy. It takes work on your part. It takes planning for each week and planning for each year. It takes commitment to give it your best week after week, but isn't that what our Saviour expects from me every day, deserves from all of us all the time?

I didn't know exactly what to expect when I began teaching Sunday School at Beacon Baptist Church in the 1980-81 school year. I agreed to come in as an assistant teacher to a man who would go to the mission field within a year. That first class was half of the junior department of the Sunday School at the time, the fourth, fifth and sixth grade boys. After their time in this class they would join the teen group. They needed to prepare for that level and beyond. The girls were the other half of the department and devoted women taught them every week.

The curriculum called for one year in the five books of Moses, another in the balance of the Old Testament, and a third learning the New Testament, using Accent publications. Jim Rice was the teacher, and another veteran, Lee Vestal and I were his assistants. There was a large bus ministry in that era and eventually the class grew to 55 students. It resembled a lecture hall and the room was very crowded. There were rows of old-fashioned student desks and the aisles were filled with folding chairs!

But a building program was in place in our growing young church that resulted in the addition of six separate rooms for the junior department and other classes as well. Bruce Councilman and I became the teachers for the sixth grade only while four other men taught the other two grades. In the sixth grade we were responsible for teaching boys the New Testament, giving them a foundational understanding that each could build upon during a lifetime of study. It was not the last Sunday School class they would join, so it had to be used to prepare them for what God had ahead for them. I firmly believe students perform to the level of your expectations. If you challenge them to learn more, they will learn more.

---

*[42] And daily in the temple, and in every house, they did not cease **teaching** and preaching Jesus as the Christ.—Acts 5:42 (Emphasis added)*

Two Goals

It was not our purpose to take a pitcher of facts and pour it over their heads to get our students wet. We wanted to instill in them, 1--an enthusiasm for God's Word and, 2-- the habit of reading it--daily. If we could accomplish that in one year, our students will have won--and we will have accomplished our two goals.

The first quarter was entitled *Living in God's Family* and involved a summer of teaching the basic principles of the faith, doctrines of the church, and the attributes of God. About the time the regular school year started, the fall quarter was the *Early Life of Jesus*. The winter quarter was the *Later Life of Jesus*. The spring quarter was about *The Early Church*. Then the boys graduated to the teen group.

That was the plan we were handed. Over the years that plan has been modified to ensure that we actually completed a study of the entire New Testament in the allotted 52 weeks. The calendar for the 2023-2024 year is included on the next three pages with the quarterly titles in the last column. On the years with 53 Sundays we add an additional week to Lessons 44 and 45, the letters to churches. That allows more time in Romans and individual attention to all of Paul's 13 letters. We prepare this lesson plan near the end of each year and provide copies to the pastors as an aspect of accountability.

In my business practice I thought in terms of goals, strategies and tactics. In some ways those same concepts can be applied in Sunday

School, as well as teaching, learning and many other aspects of our lives.

Again, our goals are two-fold. We want the students to complete the year with an enthusiasm for God's Word and the habit of reading it daily.

2023-2024 6ᵗʰ GRADE BOYS SUNDAY SCHOOL PLAN

Week Number	Sunday Date	Card Mails	Card Arrives	Scripture on Postcard	Picture on Postcard	Lesson Title and Events
1	6/4/23	5/25	5/31	Ephesians 2:1-10	Bible	*Living in God's Family* #1, Salvation
2	6/11	5/31	6/6	Psalm 139:1-18	Planes over Niagara Falls	2 Holiness, Three Omnis of God
3	6/18	6/7	6/13	Romans 12:1-11	Bear	3 Serving God In the Church
4	6/25	6/14	6/20	2 Timothy 2:1-7	Rocket Launcher	4 Soldier, Farmer, Athlete
5	7/2	6/21	6/27	Luke 19:1-10	Frog/Mouse	5 Giving to God, Meeting Zacchaeus
6	7/9	6/28	7/5	John 3:1-8, Gal.5:22-23	Watermelon	6 Holy Spirit, Fruit of the Spirit
7	7/16	7/5	7/11	I John 1:1-10; Is.6:1-9	Cruiser (ship)	8 Fellowship with God
8	7/23	7/12	7/18	2 Tim. 2:15, 3:15-17	Bible	9 Studying the Bible, Pastor visits
9	7/30	7/19	7/25	Romans 13:1-7	Flag	11 Forgiveness and 12 Government
10	8/6	7/26	8/1	Deut. 6:1-9, Prov. 4:1-5	Cartoon	13 Getting Along with Parents, Spanking
11	8/13	8/2	8/8	Luke 1:46-56	Puppies	*Early Life of Christ* #1, Words From Heaven
12	8/20	8/9	8/15	Luke 2:1-20	Manger (art)	2 Jesus' Birth From Luke and Matthew
13	8/27	8/16	8/22	Luke 2:52	Polar Bear on ice	3 Jesus' Childhood, In the Temple
14	9/3	8/23	8/29	I Cor. 10:13	Gun Deck	4 Baptism, Temptation; **Attendance Awards**
15	9/10	8/30	9/5	John 1:35-41	Ostrich	5 Meet the Disciples, 1ˢᵗ miracle
16	9/17	9/6	9/12	John 3:1-16	Deer	6 Nicodemus, 10 Great Things about John 3:16

Week Number	Sunday Date	Card Mails	Card Arrives	Scripture on Postcard	Picture on Postcard	Lesson Title and Events
17	9/24	9/13	9/19	John 4:4-16	Artwork/ Jesus	7 Woman at Well
18	10/1	9/20	9/26	Matt. 5:1-12, Luke 6:12-19	Fall Leaves	8 Sermon on Mount, The Beatitudes
19	10/8	9/27	10/3	Matthew 13:1-23	Sower (art)	9 Parables by Sea
20	10/15	10/4	10/10	Luke 5:1-11	Fish Jumping	10 Power over Nature
21	10/22	10/11	10/17	Mark 5:1-20	Gadara	11 Power over Demons
22	10/29	10/18	10/24	Luke 17:11-19	Thank You Birds	12 Power over Leprosy
23	11/5	10/25	10/31	Matthew 10:1-17	Big Ape	13 Power to Disciples
24	11/12	11/1	11/7	Matthew 16:13-16	Fox among Hounds	*Later Life of Christ* #1, Jesus is the Christ
25	11/19	11/8	11/14	Luke 15:1-7	Wildlife Birds	2 The I AMs begin; Seeker of Lost
26	11/26	11/15	11/21	John 6:44-51	Bread	3 Bread of Life
27	12/3	11/22	11/28	John 9:1-5	Seaside Sunset	4 Light of World **Attendance Awards**
28	12/10	11/29	12/5	John 10:1-11	Ram	5 Good Shepherd
29	12/17	12/6	12/12	John 11:25-26	Earth Night	6 Resurrection & The Life
30	12/24	12/13	12/19	Mark 11:7-11	Snowman	7 Christ is King; Milk & Christmas Cookies
31	12/31/23	12/20	12/27	Matthew 24:37-39	Cowboy	8 Jesus is The Coming One
32	1/7/24	12/27	1/2	Luke 22:1-13	Garden	9 Jesus Kept The Passover
33	1/14	1/3	1/9	Luke 22:47-62	Lake	10 Jesus Stood Trial 3 Jewish, 3 Roman
34	1/21	1/10	1/16	Matthew 27:33-50	Church at Sunset	11 Crucifixion
35	1/28	1/17	1/23	Matt. 27:62 thru 28:15	Flowers	12 Resurrection
36	2/4	1/24	1/30	Acts 1:1-11	Bulls	13 Ascension, Left With a command

Week Number	Sunday Date	Card Mails	Card Arrives	Scripture on Postcard	Picture on Postcard	Lesson Title and Events
37	2/11	1/31	2/6	Acts 2:1-8	Callaway Chapel	Early Church #1, Church Begins
38	2/18	2/7	2/13	Acts 5:1-11	Blue Angels	2 Church Grows
39	2/25	2/14	2/20	Acts 9:1-19	Saul on Road to Damascus	3 Gospel to the Gentiles
40	3/3	2/21	2/27	Acts 11:19-26	Paul's Trips Map	4 Antioch Missionaries **Attendance awards**
41	3/10	2/28	3/5	Acts 15:36-41	Parthenon Today	5 Church to Europe; Philippian jailor
42	3/17	3/6	3/12	Acts 17:1-4	Jelly Beans	6 Church spreads in Europe
43	3/24	3/13	3/19	Acts 19:8-10, 23-41	Happy Birthday	7 2 years in Ephesus, Birthday Cookies/Milk
44	3/31	3/20	3/26	I Corinthians 15:1-4	Plane and ship	8 Letters to Churches
45	4/7	3/27	4/2	Galatians 1:1-9	Tiger in tree	8 Letters to Churches (continued)
46	4/14	4/3	4/9	Acts 21:6-12	Lion	9 Paul Before Kings, Agrippa
47	4/21	4/10	4/16	Acts 26:27-32	Lighthouse	10 To Rome, Prison Epistles
48	4/28	4/17	4/23	I Timothy 2:1-4	Airplane Landing	11 Paul's Last years, Pastoral Epistles
49	5/5	4/24	4/30	Jude v20-25	Mother's Day (Our mothers)	12 James, Peter, Jude; Begin review
50	5/12	5/1	5/7	2 Timothy 3:1-17	Ephesus Coliseum	13 Revelation; more Review the study list
51	5/19	5/8	5/14	Rev. 1:19; 22:18-19	Ark	51st Homecoming Sunday; No class
52	5/26/24	5/15	5/21	Psalm 1	Mountain Lake	Final review; Exam **Attendance awards**
53		5/22	5/30	Proverbs 3:5-6	Covered Bridge	Farewell message
54		5/29	6/4		Giraffe Photo Bomb	Alumni Challenge

One Strategy

In short, our strategy is to have a Word-centered Classroom. Students and teachers read the word aloud in class to each other. The class is Word-centered. We tell the students, with great respect for what prior Sunday School classes have taught, that from our initial class we have put the crayons, scissors and paste away, the colorful flannelgraphs, too, as wonderful as they were for communicating God's Word. Students read God's Word, hear it their ears, see it on the whiteboard, find key words in a pre-class puzzle, and discuss the Word as it is explored and explained in class. The boys are encouraged to take notes during class and sermons as well. Tactics will be unfolded in following chapters.

> Pastor Al Mohler wrote in *Tell Me the Stories of Jesus*, "Christian ministry is not about technique and it is certainly not about the latest fads or glittering programs. It is about the ministry of the Word—most importantly, the preaching and **teaching** of the Word of God. Gospel ministry and the preaching of the Word of God are not just an initial strategy—there is no Plan B. God's glory is in the preaching of His Word, and the evidence of the Word's power is a harvest of transformed lives." (Emphasis added)

This is why as Sunday School teachers we all must parallel the preaching from the pulpit. It is our one and only strategy.

Duties of a Teacher

First we must pause to examine the primary duties of the teachers. We must strive daily to be the Christian that God wants us to be. We must live each day for His honor and glory. Our spiritual condition is of paramount importance. This begins with reading the Scripture daily. My personal plan includes reading the Bible through every year.

I had read the New Testament several times, but not the entire Bible. Then one Christmas I saw that my mother-in-law had read the entire Bible 25 times. I'm thankful for a godly mother in-law. I realized that there were benefits that I had been missing without a cover-to-cover reading. I did the math and discovered that I could read three chapters each day, five when I got to Psalms, and if I didn't leave any widows hanging (a printing term from my past for fragments, one or two leftover chapters), I would finish in a year. I have used chronological Bibles that are prepared for once-a-year reading as well.

The back of my Bible has a list of the completion dates of each annual reading along with my signature. I show this to the pastors each year as an aspect of accountability, and hopefully, encouragement. Until writing this, the only others to know this were our Sunday School students during our week eight lesson, when we focus on how to study the Bible. You cannot ask your students to read the Bible every day if you are not willing to.

Commentaries, Christian biographies and other books from your church's book room should also be in your menu of study, but your focus must be on the Word of God. The old story said that the country preacher was asked about a commentary someone had given him, and responded, "The Bible sure does shed a whole lot of light on that commentary!" Think about that.

> Martin Luther wrote a letter to George Spalatin on Jan. 18, 1518 about the importance of Bible study. Here is an excerpt, "To begin with, it is absolutely certain that one cannot enter into the (meaning of) Scripture by study or innate intelligence. Therefore your first task is to begin with prayer. You must ask that the Lord in His great mercy grant you a true understanding of His words, should it please Him to accomplish anything through you for His glory or that of any other man. For there is no one who can teach the divine words except He who is their Author, as He says, '…And they shall all be taught by God.' (John 6:45, NKJV) You must therefore completely despair of your own diligence and intelligence and rely solely on the infusion of the Spirit."

That is beyond humbling. Study the Word carefully for yourself and then let it do its work in the hearts of your students. We gather in church to worship and learn more of our God. The teachers tell our testimony of salvation in the first two weeks each year. We teach as if students need salvation--and let them tell us only when they are ready. We never ask directly if they are saved, because we don't want them to feel any pressure to verbalize a false profession. We don't want them to think they are saved and be wrong. I John 5:13 tells us, "These things I have written to you who believe in the name of the Son of God, that you may know that you have eternal life, and that you may continue to believe in the name of the Son of God."

Our overarching tactical plan is two-fold to achieve the stated goals. First, we must parallel the pulpit, and secondly, we want to support what is taught at home. It is confusing to any student to hear one message from the pastor of your church or a parent and a conflicting message in Sunday School. Never contradict your pastor. Do nothing in a closet either, nothing that is shielded from your students' parents. It is said that children are God's little spies. If you misstate doctrines heard from the pulpit it is sure to be repeated, so make sure you echo the doctrine heard from the pulpit.

Many of the 52 scheduled lessons in the plan on pages 4-6 are modelled after messages from the Beacon pulpit, which we have enjoyed since 1980. I began using a notebook while listening to Pastor Barkman's sermons in 1982, in outline form. In less than a month I realized that his messages were so well-planned and clearly presented that I converted to listening then writing out the sermons in complete sentences. Many portions of those sermons have found their way to our classroom. That's also how the sermon entitled "The 10 Greatest Things About John 3:16" by Dr. Norman Marks became Lesson 16 and appears in this book. The worship service at Beacon precedes the Sunday School hour. It is remarkable how often the morning message repeats something we have covered in previous classes or had planned to present that same day. We credit that to Holy Spirit supervision and the commitment to teaching a parallel doctrine in the classroom to the one from the pulpit.

[12] For the word of God is living and powerful, and sharper than any two-edged sword, piercing even to the division of soul and spirit, and of joints and marrow, and is a discerner of the thoughts and intents of the heart.—Hebrews 4:12

What Do I Do First?

You've just been appointed to be a Sunday School teacher and you're very excited for the opportunity to serve the Lord in this way. There is a lot to do before you enter the classroom, so let's get started.

First, pray God will direct you and that the time will be profitable for your students. Let's assume you are in a graded classroom with students who have advanced from a prior grade. Obtain the roll book from the past year and pray for those students. Prepare your new roll book in advance of the class. Get the home address of each student and mail a picture post card in time for it to arrive before the first class. The appendix includes the content for the message side of each of the cards we use. A sampling of the picture side of the cards appears on the back cover as well. Both are numbered matching the week on the yearly schedule, so you can check them out together if you like. Create your own text for each week. More about the picture post cards later.

*[26] But the Helper, the Holy Spirit, whom the Father will send in My name, He will **teach** you all things, and bring to your remembrance all things that I said to you.—John 14:26 (Emphasis added)*

How Do I Prep the Classroom?

Try to be the first to arrive in your classroom, particularly if your students are children, as we are considering here. The entire environment of the classroom should make it clear that there is a prepared plan for the hour. The Scripture to be covered is always listed in the upper right corner of our whiteboard, allowing students to find their place, be ready for the lesson, without having to ask you to repeat. Words on the board, in the word search puzzle they find at their seat, in the Bible that will be read by them and spoken by the teacher, all create the repetition needed for lasting instruction. All this takes some planning, but nothing like preparing the master plan for the year. See pages 4-6. We discovered many years ago that with our assignment to teach the entire New Testament in one Sunday School year, it could not be done without prior planning. When time is limited, resolve to teach what you can—as well as you can. Write the day's subject on the board at the front of the class and the key points below that.

Be seated at the front of the classroom when your students arrive. Seeing you seated, they will likely go directly to a seat rather than wandering around. We don't use assigned seating unless that becomes necessary. Have a predetermined seat for each teacher however, usually an adult chair if there are different types of furniture in your classroom. If the class is small enough to sit around a table I recommend that. It provides a place for the Bibles and has everyone facing the group. A round table can usually seat six to eight. When we have more students we pair two eight-foot tables, creating 12 to 16 seats, again keeping everyone in the front row. We have used a semi-circle when tables weren't available or suitable but we have rarely needed more than one row.

Parents are always welcome to join the class, and occasionally one will. We have had families visit the church for the first time and come by before class to find out what is being taught to their child. We show them our annual plan and they usually go to their own class satisfied that their son will hear a Bible lesson that day. If they are local we get their home address and begin mailing weekly post cards. Then parents know exactly what their child is studying each week.

We don't do anything behind a curtain. Sometimes parents like a particular subject and will attend a class later. I have asked some parents if they would like to come back sometime. The usual response is that it is not necessary since they know what their son is learning. (Of course, everyone knows a child's fondest desire is for their parents to be in their Sunday School class!)

One further note about seating arrangements. If you need to separate two students, I suggest having the other teacher sit between them.

All your preparation for the classroom makes it clear that the teachers are prepared, a plan is in place, and everything is well organized for a good year of instruction in God's Word. When a group gathers, someone is always the first to arrive and someone will be last, but no one has to be late. Be on time.

---

[4] For whatever things were written before were written for our learning, that we through the patience and comfort of the Scriptures might have hope.—Romans 15:4

The Welcome Letter

In our first class meeting we take the roll out loud and ask each if he brought his Bible. Each student who has brought his Bible (as the first post card said to do) receives a "Ding," If any student forgets his Bible he receives a "Buzz!" Oops! We continue with the sound effects every week. Teachers engage with each student, one at a time, in an introductory way, asking them about their school, favorite subjects, preferred sports and teams, other activities, the names of their family members and pets, favorite foods or even ice cream flavor during this first roll call. Confirm their mailing address and make sure each received the first picture post card (See back cover) sometime during the previous week. We take everyone's photo to post those on the bulletin board all year, too. Confirm their birthdates. No matter where it lands on the calendar, we respond "Good, we'll celebrate that in March." Some have a quizzical look, but only rarely ask why. Because that's what we do. We schedule it near my March birthday which enables me to remember when, and Pam to have cookies ready!

We furnish and review a welcome letter that the boys are to take home with them. We use my Shutterfly.com account for prints of our photos without cost. We also order extra copies of the student photos to give to parents and grandparents in the church. They never turn them down! Here's a copy of the Welcome Letter:

<u>Welcome to the</u>
Sixth Grade Boys Sunday School Class
at Beacon Baptist Church

Your Teachers: Walt Atkins and Bruce Councilman

Our responsibilities: Faithfulness, read and study scripture, prepare for class, pray for our students.

Your responsibilities: Faithful attendance, coming eager to learn, stay alert in class, pray for your teachers.

COME WITH A PURPOSE!

What to bring: Bible and pen (You will use both.)

What not to bring: Anything else.

Refreshments: If you receive it here at church, you may eat it here.

Clean-up: Your mother doesn't work here, so clean up after yourself.

What we study: The New Testament (principles of Christian living, the birth, life, and ministry of Jesus, the early church, and the importance of a daily walk with the Lord)

Questions you should ask and answer at the end of the year:

1--If I live the rest of my life exactly as I am doing right now will my life be a triumph or a shipwreck?
2--Am I closer to God now than I was at the beginning of my sixth grade year?

If you have the right answers in 12 months, you will have used this coming year wisely and be prepared for seventh grade and beyond.

You will one day be the pastor in your own home. When your children come to you with questions about spiritual matters we don't ever want to hear that you said, "Go ask your Mother." It is your responsibility to know God's Word!

Bathroom Time: Is before class. Unless you are bleeding, do not even think of asking to leave once we have started. There is time after class.

Other first day notes:

Attendance Awards (at Beacon only)
Addresses, Birthdates, Parents' names
Phone numbers
Pictures for the bulletin board
Walt Atkins, walt@netpath.net

Things to Have the First Day

1	Bible
2	Lesson Plan
3	Whiteboard List
4	Pencils
5	Pre-class activity
6	Roll Book
7	Welcome Letter
8	

How Can I Use Humor?

One of my favorite moments in our first class of the year occurs when the younger brother of a former Sunday School student reaches our class. After the roll and introduction time, Bruce and I look at each other, smile and say, "Well, he's the last brother from this one family—and it looks like we finally got to the smart one!" We all share a good laugh, the youngest smiles, and would you like to guess what they all tell their older brothers on the way home? It gets the year off to a good start for him! Oh, and the older brothers tell us they take it in stride, because they came to understand our humor from their time in the class.

[4] For as we have many members in one body, but all the members do not have the same function, [5] so we, being many, are one body in Christ, and individually members of one another. [6] Having then gifts differing according to the grace that is given to us, let us use them: if prophecy, let us prophesy in proportion to our faith; [7] or ministry, let us use it in our ministering; he who **teaches***, in* **teaching***;—Romans 12:4-7 (Emphasis added)*

Teaching Should Be a Partnership

Before the lesson in the first weeks, all your teachers should give their testimony of salvation, one per week, as many weeks as it takes.

In my opinion, each class needs two teachers who are not related to each other. That minimizes the chance that both teachers would be unavailable on the same Sundays—not away for illness, vacations or family events. Students should see a consistent presence as a teacher. If both teachers are present it doesn't matter as much which one teaches, but a substitute, unfamiliar with the flow of the overall curriculum, the lesson of the day, and the students, will likely not be as effective.

I had thought for many years that Dwight L. Moody was somewhat the father of the Sunday School movement in America, but research for this book showed me that he credited one of his Sunday School teachers for showing him the gospel, leading to his conversion. I also learned that children began to attend Sunday School in England in the 1780s, primarily to promote literacy, using the Bible as their reading textbook. It is a vital part of church ministries today, where the Word of God is taught in earnest. Take a part in Sunday School if you have the opportunity. You will enjoy it, benefit from it, and be a blessing to others.

I've often said that in retirement, teaching Sunday School at Beacon Baptist Church in Burlington, NC is the most important thing I do, at least the most visible activity. It always was the most important, but with other things put aside, I am even more aware of it's even higher priority. Some churches have a shortage of Sunday School teachers, particularly since COVID, so I am writing this how-to book to encourage others to join in the work. There are lots of details, suggestions and thoughts that might be applicable to your effort. Select, adapt, and create things that will make your efforts enjoyable and effective for Christ.

Some churches may rotate teachers, monthly or weekly, into classrooms. But I think, particularly for younger students, both individual students and the entire class, it is best to sit under permanent teachers for the entire year.

The primary teacher relies on another teacher with a constant presence in the classroom, too. You can call that person a partner, an assistant teacher or a co-teacher, but having both in the classroom regularly is vital.

I have been blessed to serve with a great classroom partner for decades. Bruce Councilman taught often during the early years while I was required to be away from home for work, and now teaches once a month on average, again primarily if I am out of town, but not always. Over the years Bruce has taught every lesson in our New Testament curriculum. He is always prepared. At the start we tell the class that if I fall over during class that Bruce would prop me up in the corner, finish the sentence, complete the lesson, and then phone 911. We all enjoy a good laugh. (It's true, or it could be!) I call his name, and add "Mr. Faithful," every week when I call roll. Every Sunday School teacher should have such a partner in class.

Do not jump into Sunday School if you aren't serious about studying God's Word. Have I mentioned that before? Take this opportunity to obey the Great Commission, to give out the Word, teach and make disciples. If you have a burning desire in your heart to help people learn the Word of God and apply it to their lives, then you should teach Sunday School. If not, then you should try something else. If you are called to preach, of course, you should obey that call, but that is not something all believers can do.

God gave seven gifts to the church in Romans 12:4-8 (NKJV) "For as we have many members in one body, but all the members do not have the same function, so we, being many, are one body in Christ, and individually members of one another. Having then gifts differing according to the grace that is given to us, let us use them: if prophecy, let us prophesy in proportion to our faith; or ministry, let us use it to our ministering; he who **teaches**, in **teaching**; he who exhorts, in exhortation; he who gives, with liberality; he who leads, with diligence; he who shows mercy, with cheerfulness." (Emphasis added.)

*[6] Let him who is taught the word share in all good things with him who **teaches**.—Galatians 6:6 (Emphasis added)*

Teaching is Never Boring

One might suppose that it would be boring to teach the same thing over and over to new classes each year. Why would you think that? Elementary school teachers sometimes spend a career in the same grade. College professors teach the same courses semester after semester. Coaches have a different team every year with different personalities and abilities so they must adjust their coaching every year. We have an advantage in that while teaching one basic curriculum all these years, God has taught the sixth grade teachers more about His Word, so the lessons are actually different every year. We think they continue to improve as we learn more.

With our daily Bible reading, we often notice things we hadn't seen before in the Scriptures. Preparing for Sunday School also brings new things to our attention and we are better able to help students link the current lesson with earlier ones and prepare for upcoming lessons as well.

I like to relate the Bible study that teachers do to "Squeezing the Sponge." A sponge is supposed to absorb, but once it is saturated it can't absorb more. By squeezing the sponge it can absorb more. The Bible is a progressive unfolding of truth, building truth upon truth. The more we learn the more we can learn. The more we learn of God's Word, the better we are able to teach God's Word. We all need to get busy giving out God's Word, so teaching Sunday School is a good way to do it, don't you think?

The Bible is inexhaustible in its breadth and depth. You must think while you read. Ask yourself questions while you read, understand each word and phrase. We encourage our students (many times in a year) to read the Bible every day. You eat practically every day. Taking in spiritual food every day will help you to grow. Don't ask your students to do something you aren't willing to do. Read His Word and God will show you great things.

⁴ Show me Your ways, O Lord; **Teach** *me Your paths.—Psalm 25:4 (Emphasis added)*

⁹ Give instruction to a wise man, and he will be still wiser; **Teach** *a just man, and he will increase in learning.—Proverbs 9:9 (Emphasis added)*

Which Bible Should I Use?

Now a word about Bibles. All students must have an open Bible in front of them throughout the class. If possible try to have everyone using the same translation your pastor uses when preaching from the pulpit. Occasionally alternate translations provide additional insight, but a student hearing words that he is not seeing could be more confusing than enlightening. We have extra NKJV translations in the classroom cabinet in case a visitor should come without a Bible.

Parents are usually eager to have their sons use the same Bible that the pastor and his Sunday School class use, so suggest this if you hear any alternate translations during the initial class reading. The term versions is often applied to Bibles, but as a point of personal preference, in my mind there are many translations, but only one version of the Bible, so I use the word translation. After all, what do the saints in France, Japan, Russia and other places read but a translation in their own languages?

How Can I Support the Home?

Circling back to supporting what is being taught in the home, I mentioned earlier that parents are always welcome to attend the class anytime. One mother, new to the church, wanted to know what her son was studying in Sunday school, so she attended an early class. She participated, as everyone does. She enjoyed it and I invited her to come back again. She replied that she was confident that her son was in a class where he would learn a lot that year, and said she didn't need to come back! She did send us two more sons in later years—but never did attend again.

That story points to another reason parents can have confidence in your Sunday School class. They know what is being taught. How can they know what will be taught the next week? We mail a picture post card to every student—every week—telling them what will be discussed the next Sunday. Every card always includes a brief Scripture reference to be read during the week, before coming to class.

One Sunday I was passing through the Welcome Center at Beacon and overheard one parent wondering out loud what would be taught in their young child's Sunday School class. The listener had already put two sons through our class. I passed behind him, so I don't know if he had seen me, but he was quick to point out, "When your son reaches sixth grade you will have to work pretty hard NOT to know what is going on in his Sunday School class since you receive a post card every week telling you what is coming up!" That made this teacher smile. That weekly accountability is a major component of our goal to support what is being taught in the home.

There are 52 weeks in a year, occasionally with 53 Sundays, and then new graduates also receive two extra final cards. The messages for all cards are included in the appendix. Those text messages preceded by a # notation also have the picture side displayed on the back cover. Match the messages and the pictures for all cards by the numbers on both.

Many parents tell us that their sons keep collections of the cards in their bedroom. These seem especially meaningful to youngsters who rarely, if ever, receive mail, but look forward to going to the mailbox every Tuesday for their Sunday School card.

> [6] *"And these words which I command you today shall be in your heart.* [7] *You shall* **teach** *them diligently to your children, and shall talk of them when you sit in your house, when you walk by the way, when you lie down, and when you rise up. —Deuteronomy 6:6-7 (Emphasis added)*

> [6] *Train up a child in the way he should go, And when he is he old will not depart from it.—Proverbs 22:6*

How Do I Mail Post Cards?

Yes, there is a cost for these picture post cards. We have always used AmazingMail.com (now owned by xpressdocs) to print and mail. All our cards and address lists are archived there. I started using them for business many years ago, and enjoy using them for the King's business, too! Before picture post cards we typed a message, pasted on clip art, printed three-up mimeograph cards at church, added stamps, and mailed them locally.

Now AmazingMail does all the heavy lifting. Customer service there is great. We specify our mail dates and can count on those being honored. You will get the best value buying cards in quantity in advance—the very best value is when they have a sale going on. Postage rates are subject to change, but any card in your inventory mails at the original purchase price with no up-charge. Cards can expire though. My last purchase came with 26 months before expiration. Just know the policy when you purchase cards for extended use.

Enter the content on the web site for the cards you want to mail at least one day before you want them mailed. I tend to prepare ours in bunches since our address list is pretty stable. You can mail a single card or a large quantity. Your mailings can't be scheduled for mail holidays and those will impact desired delivery dates as well.

Each week we mail cards to every student, both teachers, and a pastor as a matter of accountability. If one of our pastors has a grandson in the class then he gets the cards, so he also can talk with his grandson about what he is learning. In any case, as a matter of accountability, at least one pastor gets one of our cards every week. When your card arrives you know they all have, so don't leave yourself out.

If the mail count exceeds your supply, you can add more cards at the time of need, but expect those to cost more than your bulk purchases. Ask when the next big sale is going to be. Being able to mail a single card is a great benefit when someone joins your class in mid-year. The third column of the 52-week Lesson Plan on pages 4-6 shows our mail dates. We can repeat cards, modify messages and change pictures as needed. We used to mail on Mondays and the students would receive them later in the week. We had to change to mail earlier, on prior Wednesdays. If we still mailed on Mondays USPS can't always deliver the cards prior to the class.

We recognize that adult and extended-stay classes are different than graded Sunday School classes in that students stay longer than a given year, but we believe that many of the concepts presented here can be adapted to those as well. Weekly cards could become bi-weekly or monthly cards, for example. The picture post cards are essential to our Sunday School class.

OK, one more story. One of our Beacon missionaries on furlough brought his youngest son to the Sunday School class. Since his son didn't know anyone here and had not benefitted from a traditional graded Sunday Class while the family was on the mission field, Dad decided to stay with him for that initial class. He participated, just like everyone in the class, and decided to remain with us every Sunday that he was in town until they went back to the field. He was a great blessing to the class.

We teach the attributes of God during the early lessons each year and emphasize holiness as being #1, primarily because if anything came before holiness it could be flawed. Our missionary contributed the infinitude of God as another primary characteristic. There is nothing outside of God. All is under his domain. Infinitude aids in understanding God's sovereignty, so we include it in all our teaching now alongside holiness.

When their furlough concluded and it was time to return to the mission field he wanted to complete the New Testament study with his son, so we provided a ring binder with the lesson plans and all the elements needed for the balance of the year, including every remaining post card and word search puzzle and his son's Christmas present. They reported using it for family devotions. Beacon Sunday School goes international!

---

¹ But as for you, speak the things which are proper for sound doctrine: ² that the older men be sober, reverent, temperate, sound in faith, in love, in patience; ³ the older women likewise, that they be reverent in behavior, not slanderers, not given to much wine, **teachers** *of good things— ⁴ that they admonish the young women to love their husbands, to love their children, ⁵ to be discreet, chaste, homemakers, good, obedient to their own husbands, that the word of God may not be blasphemed. ⁶ Likewise, exhort the young men to be sober-minded, ⁷ in all things showing yourself to be a pattern of good works; in doctrine showing integrity, reverence, incorruptibility, ⁸ sound speech that cannot be condemned, that one who is an opponent may be ashamed, having nothing evil to say of you.—Titus 2:1-8 (Emphasis added)*

Before the Lesson Begins

When our students arrive at the classroom they always find a puzzle at every seat. Typically it is a word search puzzle using terms from the Bible lesson. These are ideal since all the information needed to solve it is provided. (The Year in Review puzzle is included in the appendix.) They will see the same words in Scripture, in the outline the teacher has written on the whiteboard, and hear them when we read aloud to each other, four chances to see, hear, and read the lesson content and its core vocabulary. Repetition is important. We ask students to read the Bible carefully and require participation by everyone in the classroom, no exceptions.

We say "no exceptions" to reading out loud by every student, which gives the opportunity to relate one of the greatest Sunday School stories we know. One year a student reached the sixth grade who could not read. He could not read "cat." Bruce sat next to him the entire year. The student would run his finger across the lines of his verses and Bruce would whisper each one into his ear and he would repeat it just as if he was reading it. The Scripture came in his ear initially rather than in his eye, but his mouth spoke each word to the class.

On the 52nd and final Sunday of the year, for the first time, he read an entire verse of Scripture without any prompting. I jumped out of my seat (I was younger then) and came around and hugged him. Bruce was already there, of course. Eyes were filled with tears of joy. He may have had remedial reading at school or other instruction, but it being the first time he read aloud by himself it was amazing to all of us. It was as if God looked over the battlements of heaven and said, "Oh, you want to read my Word! I'll help you learn to read." Why would Bruce sit next to one student and whisper every word to him? That's what great teachers do who love their students.

> *[11] Come, you children, listen to me; I will **teach** you the fear of the Lord.—Psalm 34:11 (Emphasis added)*

> *[58] Therefore, my beloved brethren, be steadfast, immovable, always abounding in the work of the Lord, knowing that your labor is not in vain in the Lord. —I Corinthians 15:58*

Special Lessons & Events

Lessons 5, 8, 10, 16, 29, 41, 50 and 52 are eight among 14 that all have special elements or a twist that was designed to catch the students' attention in an unusual way, or just be especially meaningful and memorable for them. These eight pop up on the calendar regularly.

Six events on the calendar need little explanation, particularly the quarterly breaks (Lessons 14, 27, 40 and 52) with the attendance awards. More later about the Final Exam, also in Lesson 52. Lesson 30 concludes with an after- class Christmas party where the boys get to tell about a gift they are *giving* to someone. Each receives a new baseball from their teachers. Lesson 43, when we celebrate all our birthdays, again after class, falls in that group. So let's now take a close look at those first eight.

Lesson 5, The Wee Little Man

This is a lesson straight from the Beacon pulpit, from Nov. 10, 2013. Jesus came through Jericho to see one man. Luke, who loves detail as much as anyone, tells us in chapter 19 of his gospel about, 1—The seeking Saviour (v1,10), 2—The seeking sinner (v2-4), 3—The personal rendezvous (v5-6), 4—The religious reaction (v7), 5—The unrecorded conversation (doubtless Jesus was personal in His approach, but God chooses not to reveal the conversation), 6—The outward response (v8), 7—The Divine declaration (v9-10). I had wondered why Dr. Luke was specific to name the tree Zacchaeus climbed to see Jesus. When I researched the sycamore tree I found it to be a tree with many branches, ideal for climbing—perfect for energetic boys! Many interesting points are in this man's salvation story.

Lesson 8, Pastor Joins Us!

Lesson 8 is Studying the Bible. We go around the table reading off the names of every book in the Bible. We emphasize that it is one book, with one author, who moved 44 human authors to write the 66 books across 2000 years and it fits together like it was written in one sitting. The mantra of (1-1-44-66-2000), helps students remember. It is a God-breathed book. It does not *contain* the Word of God, it *IS* the Word of God. It is free from error and does not contradict itself. When God includes proper names those are real people, real events and real places.

We introduce the sixth graders to a three-point plan for Bible study. First, when the Bible can be taken literally it should be taken literally. Second, it is a progressive unfolding of truth as God builds truth upon truth through the text. Third, if New Testament instruction changes your opinion about something you thought you understood from the Old Testament, go with what the New Testament teaches. Many saints have a longer list of considerations when studying Scripture, but 11 and 12 year olds can work with those three now and add other factors as they continue in the Word.

The special event of this lesson is that we invite Pastor Barkman to join us for much of the class. Senior pastors often have only limited opportunity to engage with the youth of a church, but he has joined our classes for so many years that he knows them and they know him better as they continue to worship at Beacon. Pastor explains his responsibility for personal Bible study and family devotions, how he prepares his pulpit sermons, and his thoughts on the most reliable Bible translations. Everyone enjoys his annual visit. It is one of our best classes of the year.

Lesson 10, Getting Along with Parents—Enthusiastically

God has established many things for the benefit of His children. He has established the Church, human government, and the family among those things. In Ephesians 6:1-3, Paul writes "Children, obey your parents in the Lord, for this is right. Honor your father and mother, which is the first commandment with promise: that it may be well with you and you may live long on the earth." When I spot a silver-haired man walking down the street, I always think he must have obeyed his parents!

That passage in Ephesians was quoting Exodus 20:12, the fifth of the 10 commandments. Children need to learn it's meaning and importance to them. If they expect to have children who will obey them as parents one day, they should learn to honor their own parents first. This does not mean mere obedience, but requires a willing obedience. They need to understand that God included corporal punishment in His plan. Modern society scoffs at the practice of spanking children and has turned from the practice, but it remains in the Bible as part of our parenting responsibilities.

God has given discipline by one's parents as a gift to children, so parents should not steal this valuable gift from them. Society has depicted spanking as violent and complains that it teaches children to be violent.

We share with the class the particular method our family used with our daughter, who did not grow up to be violent. In fact, she graduated high school, earned a college degree and a Masters, married and served the Lord in missions for 17 years, including time in Siberia and St. Petersburg, Russia. (Pastor Barkman even visited them there to conduct meetings with Thomas for Russian pastors.) Cristy and her family of six now live in South Dakota, where husband Thomas is an associate pastor.

Scripture exhorts children to listen, to learn, and to obey, not grudgingly nor half-heartedly, but with enthusiasm. The Bible includes the parental responsibility to teach, live a Christ-like example before their children, and raise them with discipline. Most parents love their children enough to tell them "no" at certain times, something children can and should also learn to appreciate. Here's one example.

One of our daughter's classmates was inviting others to a social event and we told her "no," she couldn't go. The family had committed to other plans and honoring that commitment was more important for her than the other event. Other parents also didn't want their daughter to attend. We found out later that they denied their daughter from going after asking "What is Cristy doing? Are her parents letting her go?" Our daughter had a testimony of obedience that mattered. That was good for all of us to know. Students can establish a reputation for obedience.

Our family's discipline was designed to be parallel to God's plan for salvation, employing confession, repentance, submission (where Jesus substitutes Himself taking our place), administration, and restoration, all similar to moments in conversion. Here's a summary of some key points we include about parenting, discipline and enthusiastic obedience.

1—The goal is restoration.
2—Spanking is under attack by people who can't abide Biblical instruction (Proverbs 13:24) to withhold not the rod from the child. God has ordained this for the child's character development. It is his God-given right to benefit from discipline. Parents should not withhold that part of God's plan for their children.
3—There are other ways to succeed with corporal punishment.
4—There is no need for violence, anger, blood, or injury present in the spanking situation.

5—Privacy is the best setting, it is not a public event.

6—Most parents love their children enough to discipline them in some way. The punishment should fit the offense. It doesn't always require a spanking. Not all offenses reach that level. Punishment should fit the offense. It can simply be a loss of certain related privileges, for example, for small offenses.

7—A neutral object is best for applying the spanking. Our hands are used to love our children. No parent would ever want their child to shrink back in fear when you approach one with an open hand. (Better to apply the board of education to the seat of instruction!)

8—One stroke with a wooden spoon is likely all that is needed, because correction has clearly already occurred when the child submits for the administration. Spank, then forgive. I have heard psychologists say that one blow, two at most, satisfies the child's conscience, knowing that they have been punished.

9—We conclude by reminding the class again that this lesson was full of Scripture, especially the responsibilities for both parents and children. Modern society has turned its back on the Bible. This small part of the curriculum is important because it helps students understand discipline and punishment— from a Biblical perspective—and arms them against society's misinformation when it comes at them in future years.

Several parents have attended this class through the years and expressed gratitude for the instruction the Bible provides.

---

*[11] **Teach** me Your way, O Lord, And lead me in a smooth path, because of my enemies. —Psalm 27:11 (Emphasis added)*

Lesson 16, The 10 Greatest

Things About John 3:16 (NKJV)

Probably the most famous verse in all the Bible, John 3:16, rolls off the tongue of most believers with ease. It's called the gospel in a nutshell with good reason. We read and discuss the entire chapter and then transition to the whiteboard. Group by group, the teacher encircles the words, spaced apart for easy circling on the board. Here are the individual elements identified in a sermon by Dr. Norman Marks, which is rendered here as it appears in my sermon notebook. Students never look at John 3:16 the same way again after this lesson.

For God	The Greatest One
so loved	The Greatest compassion
the world	The place of the Greatest need
that He gave	The Greatest benevolence
His only begotten Son	The Greatest Gift
that whoever	The Greatest invitation
believes	The Greatest response
in Him	The Greatest object of faith
should not perish	The Greatest escape
but have everlasting life.	The Greatest Hope, Promise & Blessing

A sermon by Dr. Norman Marks, at the 1985
Bob Jones University Bible Conference

Copied from my sermon notebook (Tape recording heard July 4, 1986)

This is a text we all know. Jesus is explaining to Nicodemus that as Moses lifted up the serpent in the wilderness He must be lifted up. 1—God Himself we see here, the **greatest One**, eternal, the greatest being. Today's generation doesn't know God well. He is sensitive, severe, tender, loving, kind. See Genesis 3:8-10 where God seeks a shamed sinner. Adam wasn't seeking God, He was seeking man. In Genesis 12 Abraham is brought from pagan to servant by God's mercy. In Psalm 103 we see the Redeemer who heals, satisfies, and in verses 12-13 removes our transgressions. He pities his children. We deceive ourselves about our sin.

2—The **greatest compassion**. God is love. He loved us and sent His Son for us. We love our children and some day they understand and love us back. God is the first mover in this love relationship. Don't ever forget where God found you. 3—The **place of the greatest need**, the world, a place of continual evil. See Galatians 1:4. The world makes a stronger appeal for our soul than ever before, with more tools to do it. Only eternity will reveal how much of the philosophy of this age and the evil and the scum and the filth of it has been put into the living room of Americans by television alone. See Ephesians 2. We're in this world, but not of it. I John 5:19. God allows wickedness to go only so far. Thank God for what He has done for you. Know the Lord and know that you know Him. Have a desire to live for Him and not embarrass Him. May this be so real that you have to share it.

4—The **greatest benevolence**. There was a Saviour even before there was a single sinner. 5—The **greatest gift**, the Son. See 2 Corinthians 9. Paul appeals to a church stuck on itself and cheap and tawdry about giving. He reminds them of the unspeakable gift. The best preacher ever couldn't convey this gift. 6—The **greatest invitation**, whosoever.

The Bible is not exclusive. Only Christ-rejecters are excluded and that is because they exclude themselves. See 1 John 2:2. Jesus died for all. He saves all who will have Him.

7—The **greatest response**, believeth. See Hebrews 11:6. Believe that God is and that He rewards those who diligently seek Him. My heart breaks when I meet a man who is so smart or too philosophical to come to God by faith. God will pour out blessings by the bushel if a man will just believe and come by faith. Romans 10:17, and 1:17 and Hebrews 10:38. We are saved by faith and live by faith. We have had it too good in this nation and we don't live by faith as we once did. I believe America is headed for a rude awakening in a time of hardship. I wonder if it will stir a faith in God. American people have lost their faith in God. They have lost faith in their leaders. They have lost faith in their pulpiteers. Most preachers aren't worth our faith today. Stick by the Book preachers.

8—The **greatest object of faith**, Jesus. See John the Baptist's enthusiasm for the Lord. He only lived for God. Acts 4:12, John 3:36. 9—The **greatest escape**, shall not perish. We deserve hell and receive heaven. We don't preach enough on hell today. Nobody spoke more about hell than Jesus did. Mark 9:41-50, Luke 16. Hell is a terrible place. Who is Houdini compared to the escape we believers make from hell? 10—The **greatest hope, promise and blessing**, the everlasting life. We have eternal security. See Luke 10:20, John 5:24. There are the 10 greatest things about John 3:16. If you aren't saved yet, be saved today. Take the Christ of John 3:16.

---

*[1] You therefore, my son, be strong in the grace that is in Christ Jesus. [2] And the things that you have heard from me among many witnesses, commit these to faithful men who will be able to **teach** others also.—2 Timothy 2:1-2 (Emphasis added)*

Where Do I Find Sermons?

Since 2000, millions of people in countries around the world have visited SermonAudio.com to learn more about God and His Word through its over 2.6 million online sermons. You will find sermons by 44,067 speakers, organized by book, chapter, and verse, in video or audio or both formats.

Sermons are available in many popular foreign languages including Chinese (5,167 Sermons), French (2,614), German (3,239), Korean (1,484), Portuguese (2,119), Russian (579) and Spanish (43,370). In all, sermons are available in 55 foreign languages from Afrikaans (722) to Zulu (19).

"We have enjoyed a fruitful relationship with SermonAudio for many years, and continue to be immensely blessed by this ministry. We enjoy seeing the many sermon downloads from all across the USA and the world, and are especially encouraged by the numerous email contacts we receive from listeners who write to ask questions, or just to encourage us. We praise the Lord for making this internet service available to us and for being able to recommend it to others."
—Gregory N. Barkman, Pastor, Beacon Baptist Church

Sermons that could be
Sunday School Lessons

Here's space to note pulpit messages which could become Sunday School lessons for your class:

	DATE	SUBJECT	SCRIPTURE	SPEAKER
1				
2				
3				
4				
5				
6				
7				
8				

Lesson 29, I AM the Resurrection and the Life

Jesus is life itself to believers. As we studied the "I AMs" of Scripture we come to the one that led directly to His crucifixion. He told Lazarus to come out of the tomb and he did—somehow. How? Well, he came out wearing his grave clothes. He would need them again after all. Here's where the boys enjoy having a chance to act out how they think he managed to come to his feet and walk out to the crowd. It's usually pretty funny to see how they imagine the scene, and one that helps them remember this "I AM."

Lesson 41, The Philippian Jailer

Ask me about folks in the Bible I'm looking forward to meeting in Heaven and I'll add two to the traditional lists who are notable for me. They are the Philippian Jailer and Malchus. God has men in all walks of life who are His servants and also perform their civic duty or job. Here are 10 things that the jailer did that make him remarkable. This is another lesson taken from the Beacon pulpit of Sept. 15, 1991. His story comes from Acts 16.

1—He was **at his post** while prisoners were in his jail. He had a home, but it was midnight and he was sleeping at the prison. (V27)

2—He **knew his job responsibility**. When the earthquake popped the doors of the prison open he thought the prisoners had escaped, drew his sword, willing to administer the punishment required if they had. (v27)

3—Hearing Paul, **he ran directly to the source of truth**. Most unsaved people would run to their unsaved friends. (v29)

4—He **asked the question of the ages**, "Sirs, what must I do to be saved?" (v30)

5—He **took the men to his home**. (v32)

6—He **washed their stripes**. (v33)

7—He **believed** (v34), and **evangelized his household.** (v33)

8—He and his family were **obedient to God in baptism** (v33)

9—He **fed the prisoners**. (v34)

10—He **took the prisoners back to the prison**. (v35) He didn't say, "Oh, you nice little Christian boys, you go your way now and I'll explain it to the magistrates tomorrow." Thereby, **fulfilling his civic responsibilities**.

When we finish our study of the text, we ask the students to tell us the name of the Philippian jailer. They search carefully, but of course, they can't find his name because it isn't mentioned. To help them remember this man and his faithfulness we go into an elaborate explanation of how their teachers had researched the historical records, and discovered his name. After all everybody had one back then. We lay it on pretty thick so they know we are having fun with them for a memorable point. Then we ask if they want to know his name. They always say they do. Then after a dramatic pause, we tell them his name…is Bubba!

We add that if they do their own research in future years and find different information, to please come and tell us what they have learned so we can make a correction. We're still waiting. Years later students have told us they remember well the Biblical account of the Philippian jailer—and his name! Some years ago the annual NC Christian Schools State Bible Quiz competition stopped for a moment when an anonymous senior boy in the audience shouted "Bubba" at the wrong time. Oops!

Oh, and Malchus, you ask? Well, Peter drew a sword and cut off the right ear (John 18:10) of Malchus, the high priest's servant. I'm told that head wounds bleed profusely. When he arrived home his family likely asked, "Daddy, why are you covered in blood? Are you all right?" What a story he could tell. Do you think he might have become a believer after Jesus tenderly (Luke 22:51) restored his severed ear? I hope so. I'd like to hear Malchus re-tell the event. (That was covered in Lesson 33.)

---

[28] *Him we preach, warning every man and **teaching** every man in all wisdom, that we may present every man perfect in Christ Jesus.—Colossians 1:28 (Emphasis added)*

Lesson 50, The Year In Review

During the year the students learn that there will be a final exam at the end which they have to pass to be promoted to the seventh grade. We tell them that there are only seven questions. We want students to focus all through the year. We also assure them that they will pass it, because they are good students, have been well-taught at home, and have paid close attention during the year.

Students receive a copy of this review sheet with the vocabulary words from the year. We let them know what we expect of them. They should be able to say a sentence or a paragraph about each item on the list, not a doctoral thesis, just a sentence will do. These are the words they heard in class and will hear from the pulpit, and future Sunday School teachers, as they continue to study the Bible. We present copies of the list to both parents (See post card #51.) as another part of the accountability process. That gives parents a chance to review with their sons, or be available to answer their questions about any words.

*[12] So **teach** us to number our days, That we may gain a heart of wisdom.—Psalm 90:12 (Emphasis added)*

The Review Sheet

Spiritual birth
Sovereignty of God
Regeneration
Justification
Sanctification
Glorification
Attributes of God
Holiness (#1)
Infinitude
Omnipotence
Omniscience
Omnipresence
Grace
Mercy
Peace
Strength-soldier
Endurance-farmer
Discipline-athlete
Giving to God
Tithing
Worship
Baptism
Lord's Table

Fellowship
The Holy Bible
   (1-1-44-66-2000)
Bible Study(3 rules)
Serving/Gifts
Forgiveness
Citizenship
Parents, family,
   Spanking
Prophesy of
   Messiah
Sacrifices
Birth of Jesus
Jesus' Childhood
Luke 2:52
Temptation
Sin
Ministry
First miracle
Nicodemus
John 3:16 (10
   Great Things)
Woman at the Well

Sermon on Mount

Olivet Discourse

The Beatitudes

Parables

Power over nature

Power over demons

Power over leprosy

Great Commission

Jesus is the Christ

Seeker of the lost

Bread of Life

Light of the World

Good Shepherd

Resurrection & Life

Jesus is King

Coming Again

Passover

Arrest

Trials

Crucifixion

Resurrection

Ascension

The early Church

Pentecost

Holy Spirit

Fruit of the Spirit

Persecution

Dispersion

Paul's conversion

Gentiles

Pharisees

Sadducees

Antioch

Accountability

Paul and Barnabas

John Mark

Paul and Silas

Missionary trips

Philippian jailer

(10 things)

Shipwreck

Letters to Churches

Letters from Prison

Letters to Pastors

Paul before Kings

Agrippa

Armor of God

(Eph. 6:11-17)

Doctrine

Daily Walk

False teachers

Revelation Prophecy

Blessing/Warning

The Bible &

Your Life

The final exam

Lesson 52, The Final Exam

All year the students have known of this Final Exam. That knowledge and the time spent recently reviewing what they have learned comes full circle today. If they had seen the list of topics and vocabulary words at the beginning of the school year they might have thought they could never master all those things. But now they realize that they have grown in their knowledge of Scripture and their God, as revealed therein. They have used the year wisely and built a base that will serve them well as they learn more in the years ahead. It is important to let students know what they have learned.

Upon arriving for the last class of the year, each student finds a sealed envelope at his seat—with their name. The seal reads, "DO NOT OPEN UNTIL INSTRUCTED TO DO SO." Seven questions were promised. And the Scripture today provides those seven in the form of the seven tests of salvation presented in I John 1. We read and review each test in class and encourage the students to show this lesson to their parents and review it with them. In short, once the envelopes are opened it takes about 20 seconds for the students to realize that they have been had!

After class, we enjoy some homemade cookies and milk and talk with them individually and as a group. We tell each student the origin and meaning of his name and give him a Scripture verse that declares the character quality their name represents. We tell them who their teachers will be for the next year and that they will learn much from the next class. We remind them again that they have been good students and that they are well prepared to learn more and apply it to their young lives. Then we tell them that we have taught them all we know—and they have to GO!

The full text of the "Final Exam' is included in the appendix. So if you're ready to end the suspense of this final Lesson 52, look there. Students are cautioned not to discuss the final exam with any future students. So far, that has worked.

My Special Lessons and Events

Month	Lesson	Event
JAN		
FEB		
MAR		
APR		
MAY		
JUNE		
JULY		
AUG		
SEPT		
OCT		
NOV		
DEC		Christmas Party

How Do Students Take Notes?

We encourage students to take notes in Sunday School and on sermons in all worship services. Writing the date of each sermon in the margins of the Bible, next to the pastor's Scripture text, enables finding the notes in the accumulated notebooks years later. Taking notes on loose pages and keeping them organized is difficult to manage for the long term, so to help our students get started we have been furnishing students in recent years with a blank ruled notebook, a bound book, sufficient to last for many months or more.

We place three labels on the notebooks. The student's name and the title appear on the front cover. Two other labels are added inside.

<u>Label on the Inside Front Cover</u>

Presented by
your 6th grade teachers,
Walt Atkins and Bruce Councilman
"Study to show thyself approved unto God,
a workman that needeth not to be ashamed,
rightly dividing the word of truth."
II Timothy 2:15 (KJV)

<u>Label on the Last Page</u>

When you have filled this notebook
please select a notebook style you
will enjoy the rest of your life.
Remember, your family, other students,
and someday even your own children,
may follow your diligent example.

---

[20] *Now then, we are ambassadors for Christ, as though God were pleading through us: we implore you on Christ's behalf, be reconciled to God.—2 Corinthians 5:20.*

How Do I Invest in My Students?

Make it a practice to invest in your students. This can come in many forms and many ways.

The regular Sunday School post cards is one way you invest in your students, become a part of their lives. One saying I have is that, "Things that interest my friends interest me." Find out what interests each one.

In the early years we took the class to college football and baseball games, wrestling matches and the like. They were well-behaved and enjoyed the time together as a class. We had two rules. We sit together and no one leaves the group by themselves. No one else leaves the group until the other two have returned. It's self-policing that way because the boys will tell anyone they have been away too long. If we went on a Sunday afternoon after church we went to a restaurant for lunch first. We prayed, asking the blessing before we ate, and they learned to leave a tip for the server.

The leader of junior church began to organize events for the larger group so our events became more personal to each one. I enjoyed attending their school soccer games, cross country meets, football, basketball, wrestling and golf events, even pee wee football while they were our students, many more after they had moved on to higher grades. They are usually surprised and proud that their Sunday School teacher came just to see them!

There were music recitals, school plays and eventually graduations and many weddings. Sometimes it meant driving to nearby towns, sometimes to Illinois or Texas. Many had younger brothers that we would come to know and teach in later years. The students came to realize that their Sunday School teachers cared about them outside the classroom. My wife and I even hired many of them for special projects when the need arose, usually after they were gone from the class, of course. Pam and I hosted backyard fellowship meals many years and quite a few enjoyed those through the years with their families.

The point is to look for opportunities to invest your time in the lives God puts before you in the Sunday School classroom. Be a blessing to them in whatever way best fits your schedule and it will lead to a lifetime of good Christian fellowship with them and their families.

---

[16] *Let the word of Christ dwell in you richly in all wisdom,* **teaching** *and admonishing one another in psalms and hymns and spiritual songs, singing with grace in your hearts to the Lord.—Colossians 3:16 (Emphasis added)*

How Do I Get Good Behavior?

Maintaining good order in the classroom is important for all students to learn as much as possible in the short time you have with them. Disorder hinders learning. Our students see the structure in the class, know what is expected of them and are very well-behaved. I credit that to the training they have at home.

One year we were warned well in advance about a student who would be a disruption in our class. Since all our students were so well-behaved, I didn't think it would be a problem. The class was larger than usual and all went well for a while, then a few times a couple of students distracted others without being called on, you might say.

The next Sunday before class I asked for a show of hands of who planned to act up that day. Two hands went up. "OK, Joe and John, I see your hands. Anybody else? (pause) Joe and John, that's all. Thank you." During the class, sitting in the back row in the small classroom we had that year, the student we had been warned might be disruptive started a conversation with another student without being called upon.

"Stop! Hold everything! Jim, only Joe and John raised their hands and have permission to act up today. You will have to wait for another week." He knew he had been had, and never brought unnecessary attention to himself the rest of the year. By the way, Joe and John didn't take advantage of their moment either. Of course, I never asked that question again. We were able to commend that first student to the seventh grade teachers with confidence. Another by the way, we don't recommend having a back row in case you missed that point earlier.

> [26] *But the Helper, the Holy Spirit, whom the Father will send in My name, He will* **teach** *you all things, and bring to your remembrance all things that I said to you.—John 14:26 (Emphasis added)*

> [20] *And you shall* **teach** *them the statutes and the laws, and show them the way in which they must walk and the work they must do.—Exodus 18:20 (Emphasis added)*

Final Thoughts...

Since you've gotten this far, can I assume you are getting excited about teaching Sunday School? It will be a lot of work, but the reward is so great. Have you started to create something special for your students?

Great News! There is no Mandatory Retirement Age!

Prepare a plan to leave behind when you retire so the next teacher can pick up right where you left off and keep the excellence in teaching on track.

Don't repeat what we do, use it as a model for constructing your own plan.

The Socratic Method uses questions to encourage the students to think. Sometimes students are hesitant or reluctant to answer questions when we pose those. They may hesitate even when they know the answer. We often use questions as a teaching point when we are probing their prior knowledge of subject matter for that class. For example: "How many men are named James in the New Testament?" Waiting for the answer can take a moment, but when it comes--it's always right in our class. "Three," the student replies. The teacher replies, "Right, four! That is what you said, isn't it?" Smiles all around, no frowns. Two were apostles, James (brother of John and a fisherman) and James the son of Alpheus (also called James the Less), James the half-brother of Jesus, and James, mentioned once (Luke 6:16) as the father of Judas Labbaeus, also called Thaddeus. We created this style of questioning and affirmation to overcome shyness and encourage eager participation.

The first post card we send encourages students to underline words, phrases and verses in Scripture, making them easier to find again later. We mention it many times later in the year. Bruce brings his post card each week and uses the hard edge as a ruler for underlining in class. A former student first did that, so Bruce uses it to encourages others to underline, too.

Talking about various Bibles, I expressed a personal preference for the term translations over versions. For Savior I write Saviour—just me, too.

Years ago I had occasion to visit a church that gave awards for packing a pew or other special promotions. We feel that the Word of God should be sufficient reward for regular attendance. However, we realize that our sixth graders do not drive themselves to church each Sunday, so we began a quarterly award for those who attended 12 of 13 Sundays each quarter. The reward is a Snickers candy bar. FYI, bringing their Bibles counts 50% of their attendance score. (Thus it really is 24 of 26.)

We have another reward for those who attend at least 10 of the 13 weeks, meaning they have not missed, on average, more than once a month. The smaller award is a miniature Snickers bar. We call it the "Agrippa Award," for those who are ***almost persuaded*** to be in class every Sunday. In the summer quarter we chip each award one extra week, allowing for family vacations. Check Acts 26:28 for that one.

All the Scripture quoted in this book is from the New King James Bible unless otherwise noted. It's the one Pastor Barkman uses in the pulpit!

There are many sources of supplemental materials available today. We have ordered several of the colorful pamphlets from Rose Publishing (www.hendricksonrose.com.) to give to our students, usually after we have covered the subject from the Bible, but not always. These can provide excellent time lines or historical perspective, for example. The one about the Passion Week is helpful and we have used others from time to time. It makes the student feel special to receive these occasionally. The ones on Parables, Acts and Romans are worth a look, too, for New Testament studies. The Old Testament titles probably outnumber those, so you are very likely to find something special for any subject you are teaching.

Taking roll is an important point of interaction with students. Take it orally, not secretly, calling each student by name, "Mr. Johnson, are you here with your Bible?" Students don't want to be "Zapped" so they are faithful to bring a Bible. See page 14 for our sound effects. This way we emphasize bringing their Bible! Having their Bible counts for 50% alongside presence for attendance awards. Missing a Bible is half an absence.

Ok, Walt, when are you going to come into the 21st century and talk about technology? You send those picture post cards that cost money. When are you going to realize that everyone uses e-mail today? E-mail would be an excellent option for the adult or extended stay classes if you have one of those. But follow my reasoning for a minute.

The mailbox is still an important thing in America. Everyone checks theirs every day! Having mail sent to our boys—every week—is a meaningful thing. It is not a generic e-mail blast to a mailing list. It has their name alone on it. Parents often determine the suitable amount of computer time their children are allowed, so we don't want to drive students to the computer. Also, parents can see the post card more easily than their son's computer screen. Yes, parents could also receive copies of the e-mail, but the greatest impact for both the student and parents is in the mailbox. If the mailbox wasn't still vital in the American economy, why do businesses send their beautiful mail pieces to you? Because direct mail gets attention.

You have prepared your 52-week plan. You have each lesson well-planned. You're ready for the students to arrive. The Sunday School Superintendent comes through your door and tells you that the teacher from the next lower grade is sick and you will have those students, too. SURPRISE! How do you handle that? Are you prepared? Or, you teach girls and the boys class has to join you on short notice? Create your own emergency scenario.

First of all, remember to teach your lesson to your students. They are your priority. Incorporate the newcomers into your plan. Get their roll book and call roll just like you do for yours. Let the visitors know that everyone will participate fully in the class. Alternate seating the newcomers among your students with no second row if you can avoid it. Continue to call all the students by name throughout the class. Review key information from prior classes, if needed, to bring the newcomers up to speed on the current lesson. This emergency would not likely happen if every classroom had two unrelated teachers as mentioned previously, but you may have a similar situation in mind for which you could prepare.

Each year we appoint three student "experts" from our class. One student earns status as the geography expert, another the time expert, and a third becomes the math expert. The geography expert is the first student who discovers in the Scripture which way it is to Jerusalem. Look for it. It's everywhere. One student this year earned that title early because he was tipped off by one of his older brothers! The time expert can explain the difference between Hebrew time and Roman time when those appear in our text. (Hint, only one of the 66 books of the Bible uses Roman time.) (Giveaway hint, the three synoptic gospels were written at the same time, but one gospel was written at another time.) This is important because some skeptics claim a conflict in Bible time lines when comparing texts. The math expert title is earned by knowing math well. Each expert is called upon to clarify things when questions arise in their area of expertise.

I've often said that if boys would be involved in Sunday School and baseball (or soccer or another team sport) we would have fewer problems in America. I'm sure I'm right about the Sunday School part.

The Year in Review word search puzzle (in the appendix) is easily the largest of the year. Most are much smaller and usually completed shortly after the class gathers and attendance is recorded. If it encroaches on lesson time it becomes a take-home puzzle. Books of these are available and we created ones for more topics. Yes, there are CDs and web sites for techies!

If you have a burning desire to understand the Bible better teach Sunday School in your church. As a teacher you will learn more than your students. I have written this book that you may understand the benefits of a teaching ministry. Please don't be scared off by the responsibility.

Enjoy the rich experience of studying the Scriptures and being a Sunday School teacher.

Paul's instruction to a young pastor in 2 Timothy 2:2 was, "And the things that you have heard from me among many witnesses, commit these to faithful men, who will be able to teach others also." marks out the success that results from good teaching. It is effective teaching. Students should be able to tell their parents something they learned in Sunday School on the ride home or at the dinner table. We are to teach so well that our students can pass it on. Maybe one day two of our former students will succeed us as teachers.

---

15 Be diligent to present yourself approved to God, a worker who does not need to be ashamed, rightly dividing the word of truth.—2 Timothy 2:15

...and a Final List

The 10 best reasons to teach Sunday School:

1—You will learn more of God's Word yourself. (John 6:45)
2—Participate in teaching all nations (Matthew 28:19-20)
3—You study to show thyself approved unto God (2 Timothy 2:15)
4—Be a gift to the church (Romans 12:4-7)
5—Edify and encourage others (I Thessalonians 5:11)
6—Worthwhile use of your time (Ephesians 5:15-16)
7—Squeezing the Sponge allows you to learn more (Proverbs 18:15)
8—Be the clay in God's hand (Isaiah 64:8)
9—Help students understand why they believe (2 Timothy 3:16-17)
10—You're going to be there anyway! (Hebrews 10:25)

Permit me one final story. Recently a new student was visiting our class. We recognized the last name and asked him if he knew a former student by the same name. He said, "Yes, he's my Daddy." After class his father came to collect his son. They now live in another town and were back visiting family that weekend. I thanked the Dad for bringing his son to be with us that day. Dad responded, "Wouldn't take him anywhere else!" Wow, what a testimony for the power of God's Word. He knew where to send his son to study God's Word. Thank You, Lord!

---

[17] *So then faith comes by hearing, and hearing by the word of God.—Romans 10:17*

How To Be

The

SUNDAY SCHOOL TEACHER

They

REMEMBER

The Appendix

Year in Review Word Search

Antioch	Holiness	Peace
Ascension	Holy Spirit	Pentecost
Baptism	Jews	Pharisees
Barnabas	John Mark	Prophesy
Beatitudes	Justification	Regeneration
Bible	Leprosy	Resurrection
Christ	Letters	Sadducees
Citizenship	Lords Table	Sanctification
Crucifixion	Mercy	Sermon on the Mount
Dispersion	Messiah	Silas
Doctrine	Nicodemus	Sin
False Teachers	Olivet Discourse	Sovereignty
Fellowship	Omnipotence	Spanking
Forgiveness	Omnipresence	Temptation
Gentiles	Omniscience	Tithing
Glorification	Parables	Worship
Grace	Passover	
Great Commission	Paul	

Year in Review Word Search

```
S B A R N A B A S Y S O R P E L E T T E R S F R
R E S R U O C S I D T E V I L O E C A E P C O Y
P A R A B L E S O N N E B N O I X I F I C U R C
I T E M M O N G M C L O V O T S I R H C A S G M
H I H M O M I H N B W H I I N O I S R E P S I D
S T C S A N C T I F I C A T I O N S Q A E Q V F
R U A I A I O B P Q S N V A A E G E N T I L E S
O D E T S P D N O W Y N O C Z C U K N R U C N R
W E T P G R E A T C O M M I S S I O N A N G E E
J S E A E E M I E H P S T F T N E F P E R S S V
O A S B S S U L N R E I O I G A Y E I A U H S O
H O L I N E S S C F C M H T R Y R C C R R P E S
N H A Y T N G I E R E V O S Z I S E R U O L M S
M C F D O C T R I N E G T U W I P E N E D L I A
A O I S E E S I R A H P H J N O C S H E M D G P
R I D A J G N O I T A T P M E T L X Y P G D A E
K T K L E L B A T S D R O L I Q M L V L O E T S
D N N I W G N I H T I T S O C E T N E P O R R F
H A I S S E M G N O I S N E C S A V C F Q H P Q
```

*[11] For the grace of God that brings salvation has appeared to all men, [12] **teaching** us that, denying ungodliness and worldly lusts, we should live soberly, righteously, and godly in the present age, [13] looking for the blessed hope and glorious appearing of our great God and Savior Jesus Christ, [14] who gave Himself for us, that He might redeem us from every lawless deed and purify for Himself His own special people, zealous for good works.—Titus 2:11-14 (Emphasis added)*

The Final Exam

The Bible says that you can **know** you are saved. God is not the author of confusion. If you are saved and seek to make an impact for Christ, Satan will attack, to create doubt or ruin your testimony or effectiveness. **Your seven answers** to the following questions, as presented in I John, will fortify your assurance or send you to your knees.

1. **The test of obedience.**   (Now by this we know that we know Him, if we keep His commandments. I John 2:3)

2. **The test of brotherly love.**   (He who says he is in the light, and hates his brother, is in darkness until now. He who loves his brother abides in the light, and there is no cause for stumbling in him. But he who hates his brother is in darkness and walks in darkness, and does not know where he is going, because the darkness has blinded his eyes. I John 2:9-11)

3. **The test of worldliness.**   (Do not love the world, or the things in the world. If anyone loves the world, the love of the Father is not in him. I John 2:15)

4. **The test of fellowship.**   (They went out from us, but they were not of us; for if they had been of us, they would have

continued with us; but they went out that they might be made manifest, that none of them were of us. I John 2:19)

5. **The test of sound doctrine of Christ.** (Who is a liar but he who denies that Jesus is the Christ? He is antichrist who denies the Father and the Son. Whoever denies the Son does not have the Father either; he who acknowledges the Son has the Father also. I John 2:22-23)

6. **The test of perseverance.** (Therefore let that abide in you which you heard from the beginning. If what you heard from the beginning abides in you, you also will abide in the Son and in the Father. I John 2:24)

7. **The test of righteousness.** (If you know that He is righteous, you know that everyone who practices righteousness is born of Him. 1 John 2:29)

These things I have written to you who believe in the name of the Son of God, that you may **know** that you have eternal life, and that you may continue to believe in the name of the Son of God. (1 John 5:13)

And truly Jesus did many other signs in the presence of His disciples, which are not written in this book; but these are written, that you may believe that Jesus is the Christ, the Son of God, and that believing you may have life in His name. (John 20:30-31)

II John and III John were letters to friends he hoped to visit. John was the last living apostle.

God Bless you as you seek to know Jesus and to serve Him.

Your sixth grade teachers, Walt Atkins and Bruce Councilman

Our 52+2 Week Plan in Detail

**Message Side here, # indicates picture side on Back Cover
First Quarter (Living in God's Family)**

Lesson 1 Sovereignty of God

Postcard: WELCOME to the Sixth Grade Boys Sunday School class at Beacon Baptist Church. Be sure to bring your Bible and a pen. Each week you will receive a post card from your teachers with information about the next Sunday's class. There will be Scripture to read during the week. This Sunday we will get acquainted and you will learn what we will study this year. Read Ephesians 2:1-10. We often talk about "under-liners," verses your teachers have underlined in our own Bibles. It makes them easier to find again later. If your parents allow you to underline in your Bible, we think these will be verses you will refer to in the future. WELCOME!

Lesson 2 Three OMNIs of God

#Postcard: Sunday School is off to a flying start! We're already learning God's Word. We all should read it every day. The Blue Angels are soaring over Niagara Falls in this week's picture. We've studied God's mercy and grace and will next learn about His holiness, omniscience, omnipotence and omnipresence in Psalm 139.

Lesson 3 Serving God

#Postcard: Now that we have your attention…We've bear-ly gotten started with our Sunday School year, but already you have learned about God's #1 attribute, His holiness. We've studied the three OMNIs of God—His omniscience, His omnipotence and His omnipresence, as well as His mercy and grace. It's a reasonable thing to serve such a great God! That's the logical response of a grateful heart. Read Romans 12:1-11.

Lesson 4 Soldier, Athlete and Farmer

#Postcard: Do you have the strength to hold and fire one of these weapons? It takes training to do this job well. It takes courage, too, because if you carry this weapon you will be a prime target for enemy attack in response! Paul says the Christian life is like that of the soldier. We must train, be willing to endure hardship and follow orders. You can read about this in II Timothy 2:1-7, which we will discuss Sunday. If you serve your Heavenly Commander you, too, will be a target. Satan will seek to ruin your testimony and discourage you. Training faithfully now for whatever God has ahead for you is a wise thing to do. Paul also tells Timothy about the dedication of the athlete and the diligence of the farmer. We'll study all three.

Lesson 5 Giving to God

#Postcard: Sunday we will talk about values for eternity. "Only one life, 'twill soon be past. Only what's done for Christ will last." We'll meet the "Wee-Little-Man" who climbed the sycamore tree and the widow who served as a lesson for centuries. Read Luke 19:1-10. Giving to God is an act of worship. We should give as He commands. Tithing shows that we understand everything we have belongs to Him. What is your attitude toward money and things?

Lesson 6 The Holy Spirit

#Postcard: Sunday we'll learn about the third person of the Trinity, the Holy Spirit. The product of His work is called the fruit of the Spirit. It is one fruit with nine aspects. Believers have each of those nine to some degree when God regenerates our hearts. We grow more Christlike as we mature in faith. God's Word is as refreshing to our souls as a cool brook is to tired feet--or cold watermelon is to our insides! Read John 3:1-8 and Galatians 5:22-23 to prepare for Sunday. Folks in Bible times were familiar with the account of the Spirit of God filling the temple, so it was not a strange thought when believers learned about the indwelling Holy Spirit and the fruit of the Spirit.

Lesson 7 Fellowship

Postcard: Fellowship is an important part of our life as Christians. We sometimes say it is like fellows in the same ship. We serve together, rely on each other, have the same goal, and arrive at the destination at the same time. Our service to Christ and His Church has many aspects. Fellowship is a lot more than fried chicken, watermelon and youth activities. The fellows on this ship are a formidable force, working together. Friends are a strong influence in our lives. The friends sixth graders have will make a difference in their lives. The Bible tells us to be a friend, and warns about keeping bad company. Sunday we'll talk about choosing friends and Biblical fellowship. Read I John 1:1-10 and Isaiah 6:1-9. Have a great summer with your family and friends!

Lesson 8 How to Study the Bible

#Postcard: Are you reading your Bible every day this summer? Sunday's lesson will be about ways to read and study your Bible. Read it faithfully every day. If you don't understand everything you read the first, or even the second time, keep reading. Don't be discouraged. The Holy Spirit will work in you to help you understand. Pastor Barkman will join us for part of the class to tell us how he studies the Bible as well as how he prepares his sermons. Young people who want to improve their reading skills should read the Bible. It's as if God looks from Heaven and says, "Oh, you want to read My Word? I'll help you improve your reading!" Read II Timothy 2:15 and 3:15-17.

Lesson 9 Forgiveness and Good Citizenship

Postcard: This week's lesson covers two subjects, forgiveness and God's establishment of human government. Forgiveness is a uniquely Christian characteristic. Folks today commonly seek revenge when others offend them. But as Christians, we should find it much easier to be forgiving of others, since we have been forgiven so much. In Romans 13, God establishes human government. Read verses 1-7. We are to obey the authorities God has placed over us. The only exception is when man's law conflicts with God's law. Read the Word every day this summer!

Lesson 10 Getting Along with Parents

#Postcard: Sunday we'll learn about the roles God has planned for parents and children. Homes should be a harbor of growth, training and safety for all members of the family. Parents are to teach the Word. Children are to listen well and learn. Learn God's Word now so you will be prepared to teach it one day. You can't teach what you do not know! We'll also discuss spanking--and why it works! Read Deuteronomy 6:1-9 and Proverbs 4:1-5.

Second Quarter (Early Life of Jesus)
Lesson 11 Announcements from Heaven

Postcard: Cute puppies always bring a smile to our faces don't they? Students eager to study God's Word bring a smile to the face of every Sunday School teacher, too. This Sunday we begin studying the early life of Christ. One of our favorite passages in Scripture is The Magnificat, the response of Mary's heart to God. Enjoy it's majesty in Luke 1:45-56 this week to prepare.

Lesson 12 Jesus' Birth

Postcard: We've seen the promise of a forerunner fulfilled by the birth of John the Baptist. The Saviour he would tell the world about had the most unique birth in history. We'll study the birth of Jesus. It was a miracle and the fulfillment of another of God's promises to His people. Read Luke 2:1-20 this week.

Lesson 13 Jesus' Childhood

#Postcard: We've met the forerunner John the Baptist. We've learned about the miracle of the birth of our Saviour. Sunday we'll learn about Jesus' childhood. You can use Luke 2:52 as a life verse at your age, to model your life after the Saviour. Read it this week.

Lesson 14 Jesus' Baptism and Temptation

Postcard: These cannons are on the gun deck of the USS Constitution. It was made of live oak, a very hard wood. Captured British sailors had seen their shots bounce off it's sides. They asked if our ship was made of iron! That's how it got it's nickname, "Old Ironsides." Are you prepared to repel Satan's attack? Sunday we'll study John the Baptist's message, Jesus' baptism, and how Satan tempted Jesus--yet He never sinned. We'll see the three ways Satan seeks to tempt us to sin today. Read I Cor. 10:13.

Lesson 15 First Week's Ministry

#Postcard: So...you're wondering about the picture...and we wonder if you can tell us who he is on Sunday? We'll meet the first disciples, Peter and Andrew, James and John, as Jesus begins His ministry and does His first miracle. Read John 1:35-41.There wasn't room to mention it last week, but the gun deck of the USS Constitution was one floor below the main deck. The ship would rock back and forth in the water during battle. Our sailors would fire at the highest point when they wanted to knock out a mainsail and at the lowest point to pierce the enemy hull. That was marksmanship! They never lost a battle.

Lesson 16 Meeting with Nicodemus

Postcard: How many deer do you see? This Sunday's lesson is about Jesus meeting Nicodemus, a ruler of the Jews, who came to see Him one night. Why do you suppose he came at night? Why did he come alone? Who are the "we" Nicodemus mentions? Jesus addresses the need of his heart. We learn much from this encounter recorded in John 3:1-21. It includes a well-known verse.

Lesson 17 Meeting at the Well

Postcard: This week we study John 4, including the woman at the well. It is one of the clearest presentations Jesus ever made of His Deity. He couldn't have been clearer if he had handed her a business card saying "Messiah." Read John 4:4-16. Do you remember the 10 greatest things about John 3:16?

Lesson 18 Sermon on the Mount

Postcard: It's fall and the leaves are turning! This week we will study the Sermon on the Mount in Matthew 5-7. It begins with the Beatitudes, and gives us the opportunity to examine the attitudes of our heart. This is the major sermon at the beginning of Jesus' ministry. The Olivet Discourse is the major sermon at the end. Read Matthew 5:1-12 and Luke 6:12-19.

Lesson 19 Parables by the Sea

#Postcard: What is a parable? To some it is just an interesting story. Biblical parables are earthly stories with a heavenly meaning. The elements of the story are all familiar to the hearers, so those with spiritual understanding learn important lessons, then and today. Jesus used parables to reveal truth to those who had ears and hearts to receive the truth. Read Matthew 13:1-23 so we can talk about the parable of the soils. Farming sure has changed since a man could walk through his field with a sack over his shoulder and spread seed by hand. Giving out the Word of God, though, is still done pretty much the same as it was in New Testament times, by telling people we meet the truth of God's Word.

Lesson 20 Power Over Nature

Postcard: Do you have a fishing story you can tell us on Sunday? The disciples sure had a fish story to tell one day. You can read about it in Luke 5:1-11. Unlike most fish stories, their's really is true!

Lesson 21 Power Over Demons

Postcard: Sunday's lesson is one that Satan would rather you did not hear. It concerns demons. Jesus demonstrated His power over demons in a very public way. Some didn't like what happened that day at Gadara. Read Mark 5:1-20. Gadara is one of the cities of Decapolis. Do you remember how many cities were there? There were at least 16 harbors around the Sea of Galilee in that day.

Lesson 22 Power Over Leprosy

Postcard: Come this Sunday prepared to hear the praise of one very thankful man whom Jesus met and cured. Is your heart thankful for God's blessings in your life? Read Luke 17:11-19.

Lesson 23 Power to the Disciples

Postcard: In this week's lesson we will learn about the power Jesus gave to His disciples. Do you remember where to find the names of the 12 apostles? We'll find out what they were to do back then and how we can be His disciples today, too. Read Matthew 10:1-17. By the way, we thought you might enjoy seeing someone the Atkins met recently in Louisville, KY!

Third Quarter (Later Life of Jesus)
Lesson 24 Jesus is the Christ

#Postcard: Have you ever felt you were in the wrong place at the wrong time? Don't ask us how this fox ended up in the middle of these hounds. Do you notice he isn't saying much? The right place to be every Sunday is in Sunday School at Beacon, studying God's Word. This week we learn that Jesus is the Christ, the Messiah promised in the Old Testament. Read Matthew 16:13-16 this week. If a friend asked you who Jesus is, how would you answer?

Lesson 25 Jesus Seeker of the Lost

#Postcard: Do you remember the last time you lost something important to you? How did you feel when you found it? Did you share the exciting news with someone? Sunday we'll learn about the joy in Heaven when men repent of their sin and come to a saving knowledge of Jesus. Read Luke 15. This week's picture is actually a painting. Your teachers will bring a larger version of this picture to class. This picture contains five birds. It's easy to see three, can you find the other two? They aren't lost, just hidden except for close, careful viewing.

Lesson 26 Jesus Bread of Life

Postcard: As we continue studying who Jesus is, we come to the "I AMs" in the Book of John. This week we will see that Jesus is the Bread of Life. He did not just teach the way of Life. He is Life for the saved. He is God's gift, planned for His saints. Read John 6 this week. Do you remember what the name Bethlehem means?

Lesson 27 Jesus Light of the World

#Postcard: Last week we learned that Jesus is the Bread of Life. We have learned that Jesus is the promised Messiah, the Seeker of the Lost, and much more. We will continue studying the "I AMs" of Scripture for several weeks. For Sunday, read John 9 where we hear Jesus saying "I AM the Light of the World." Use this year to prepare for what God has ahead for you.

Lesson 28 Jesus the Good Shepherd

#Postcard: Now these are SOME SHEEP! Actually, they are big horn sheep. They aren't what we usually think of when we talk about sheep. We usually think of a flock of sheep and can picture the shepherd in our minds, counting them coming in and out of the sheepfold every day and leading them with his voice. We have a Shepherd who knows our names and guides our path. His words for us are in the Bible. Jesus is the Good Shepherd, as we will learn this week when we continue our study of the "I AMs" of Scripture in John 10. Read verses 1-11 this week.

Lesson 29 Jesus the Resurrection and the Life

#Postcard: As we approach Christmas our minds are drawn to the One who left Heaven's glory determined to die for the sins of men. Jesus is the Scarlet thread we see throughout Scripture, in the Old Testament promised yet concealed, and in the New Testament revealed to us. As we study the "I AMs" in the Book of John, we come next to the miracle that led directly to His death at Calvary. Jesus said, "I AM the Resurrection and the Life" when he raised Lazarus from the dead. Missionaries let others know about our wonderful Saviour! You can tell others, too. Read John 11:25-26.

Lesson 30 Christ is King

#Postcard: We trust you'll enjoy a very special Christmas Day! For this Sunday, read Mark 11:7-11 where Jesus presents Himself as King. Be a blessing to your other family members when you read Luke 2 and remember the birth of our Saviour.

Lesson 31 Jesus is the Coming One

#Postcard: What is the cowboy thinking about? Could he be considering the new year ahead? It's a real milestone as we flip the calendar from 2023 to 2024. It's a good time to plan. Take a few minutes to consider if you are closer to Christ and know Him better than you did when 2023 began. If you like the progress you are making, then set a course of continued study of the Word. We suggest daily Bible reading, a regular schedule with a goal. Sunday we will see Jesus as the Coming One--in fulfillment of Scripture. Read Matthew 24:37-39.

Lesson 32 Jesus Kept the Passover

Postcard: A fellow once wrote that we are nearer the heart of God in a garden than anywhere else on earth. Of course, we know God is omnipresent and we cannot escape His attention. But sometimes the beauty and serenity of the garden help us focus on the things of eternity. The night Jesus prayed in the garden He knew what the next day held, yet He willingly gave Himself. He prayed "not my will, but Yours, be done." Jesus was willing to die for you. Are you living for Him? Read Luke 22:1-13 to prepare for class.

Lesson 33 Jesus Prayed and Stood Trial

Postcard: Jesus was betrayed in the garden by the false disciple, denied by Peter three times, and endured six trials, three Jewish trials and then three Roman trials. Read Luke 22:47-62 before Sunday.

Lesson 34 Jesus Died on the Cross

Postcard: Jesus' death was different from all others. He was innocent and His accusers were guilty. On Calvary's cross He suffered a painful, humiliating death--and separation from the Father, something He had never known. He suffered physically and spiritually under God's judgement, as the penalty for our sin was on Him. He had no sin of His own. He died for the sins of others, but the whole world will not be going to Heaven. Who will? The Scriptures are written that we may know we have salvation. Read Matthew 27:33-50 before Sunday.

Lesson 35 Jesus Rose from the Dead

Postcard: Dr. Bob Jones Sr. said that sooner or later everyone comes to the realization that they are going to spend eternity somewhere. By the death of Jesus on the cross of Calvary we receive forgiveness for our sin. By His resurrection from the grave we receive eternal life. How wonderful it will be to praise our Saviour for eternity! Because He lives, we too shall live! Read Matt. 27:62 through 28:15.

Lesson 36 Jesus Left with a Command

#Postcard: We thought you might get a smile from this week's photo. Why do you suppose it got it's title? We're happy to report we didn't take it! It brings to mind the concept of final words. The last thing Jesus said before He returned to Heaven is in Acts 1:1-11. It's called "The Great Commission." We are to give out the Gospel to the world, starting at home. It was not The Great Suggestion. God saves whom He will and we have the privilege of telling about our wonderful Saviour. Sadly, for many, it is The Great Omission--something many neglect.

Fourth Quarter (The Early Church)
Lesson 37 The Church Begins

Postcard: This Sunday we will study the beginning of the Church and the early years of what we call "The Church Age." Read Acts 2:1-8 this week as you prepare your heart for class. The human author of the Book of Acts also addressed one of the gospels to the same person. Who wrote Acts?

Lesson 38 The Church Grows

#Postcard: Do you ever experience days when everything seems upside down? These Blue Angels are flying that way on purpose. They aren't disoriented or confused at all. When Jesus departed, the disciples were a little confused. The arrival of the Holy Spirit energized them to action. The church grew daily. Deacons were elected to take care of the daily ministries, while the disciples devoted their days to prayer and preaching. Their stand for God soon brought opposition. Satan attacked the church from outside, and, yes, even from within. One of the first deacons became the first martyr. If you stand up for Jesus today the world will oppose you, too. Read Acts 5:1-11.

Lesson 39 Gospel to the Gentiles

#Postcard: In the early days of the Church, PERSECUTION of the believers by Jewish leaders caused many of them to flee Jerusalem-- and the gospel began making its way to the uttermost parts of the earth. Sound familiar? It was called the DISPERSION and God used it for His purposes. A Pharisee named Saul was going to Damascus one day, not looking for salvation, when Jesus met him and marvelously, and permanently saved him. Read Acts 9:1-19. See you Sunday!

Lesson 40 Antioch Sends Missionaries

Postcard: The Scripture says that believers were called "Christians" first in Antioch. Paul began his first missionary trip there. His course for each mission trip is drawn on the map. He reported back to Antioch when the journey was done. Missionaries report to their sending churches today, too. Read Acts 11: 19-26.

Lesson 41 The Church Reaches Europe

Postcard: Paul's second missionary trip took the gospel to Europe. It spread from there to the rest of the world. Sunday we'll learn about the first half of that trip of 2000 years ago and meet the Philippian jailer. You'll learn why this official is one of the heroes of the New Testament and in many ways a model for us today. You will hear about the "special" research your teachers have done in this area. Be sure to read Acts 15:36-41 before class.

Lesson 42 The Church Spreads in Europe

Postcard: What youngster doesn't enjoy a fistful of jelly beans once in a while? They are colorful and so sweet to the taste. Easter is coming March 31, so you might see some of these! From our study of Scripture, we know that the celebration of Easter commemorates the Resurrection and is best represented by the empty tomb. Yes, Jesus physically, actually, bodily arose from the grave! This Sunday we'll complete our study of Paul's second missionary trip. Paul visits Athens, where people were highly educated. They thought they had all the answers, as most folks think today. Read Acts 17 to prepare for Sunday School.

Lesson 43 Two Years in Ephesus

Postcard: On his third missionary trip Paul spent two years in Ephesus. The Ephesian Christians learned to reject idols made with hands and the occult, both very dangerous things. Idol makers got mad at Paul's preaching. Folks still get mad today when someone shows them from Scripture that they are sinning. Read Acts 19:8-10 and 23-41 before Sunday. Don't forget, after class we celebrate everyone's birthday this week, too!

Lesson 44 Letters to Churches, Part 1

Postcard: We take long trips with ease in planes and ships today, but it was different in the first century. Our study of Paul's three missionary trips is complete. We are going to invest the next three Sundays in 1st and 2nd Corinthians, Galatians and Romans. Read I Cor. 15:1-4 for Sunday.

Lesson 45 Letters to Churches, Part 2

#Postcard: We learn God's truths today by reading our Bibles. Back in the early days of the Church the New Testament hadn't been written yet, so it was easy for wrong teaching to slip in. Paul's letters to churches gave the young believers good guidance. Read Galatians 1 to prepare for class this Sunday. Read the Word every day.

Lesson 46 Paul Before Kings

#Postcard: The lion is often called the "King of the Jungle" and strikes fear in the heart of men. Speaking before men in authority is sometimes compared to putting your head into the mouth of the lion. It, too, can be dangerous. God promised Paul that he would witness to kings and go to Rome. Paul relied on that promise. He would present God's Word to Roman kings, including the infamous King Agrippa, the one who uttered some of the saddest words in all of Scripture. Read Acts 26:27-32. Have you begun to see how well Scripture fits together? It is not a collection of stories, but a record of the unfolding of God's plan.

Lesson 47 Paul Goes to Rome

Postcard: Coastal lighthouses guide passing ships to safety. We have the truth of God's Word to guide us daily. Use this time in your life to prepare for what God has ahead for you. Then you can let your light shine before others and they will learn about your Father in Heaven. Paul's imprisonment continued and he suffered shipwreck, but that did not keep him from witnessing about Jesus. Of course not! This week's Scripture includes high seas adventure and reveals the power of God to complete His plan. Read Acts 27:37-44. We'll study Paul's trip to Rome and search his letters from prison, too. Be faithful.

Lesson 48 Paul's Last Years

#Postcard: Oops! Yes, the truck stopped short and was missed. The road has since been relocated away from this airport! In his final years, Paul wrote letters to Timothy and Titus, two young preachers. These are known as the Pastoral Epistles. They don't seem to be written from prison like Ephesians, Philippians, Colossians and Philemon were. We'll be Bible detectives Sunday and see if we can figure it out. Read I Timothy 2:1-4 and II Timothy 3:16-17. As we bring the Sunday School year in for a landing in a few weeks, we have a lot of Scripture to cover to complete our study of the New Testament. Give it full power!

Lesson 49 James, Peter and Jude

Postcard: Be thankful for a Godly mother! Let this card be all the reminder you need that Mother's Day is coming up on Sunday, May 12. Make sure it is a memorable day for Mom. Sunday, we'll continue in letters, those by Peter, James and Jude. We'll also begin a review of what we have studied this year to help you prepare for a lifetime of service for Christ. Remember Father's Day is coming June 16. Read Jude, v20-25.

Lesson 50 Revelation

Postcard: Sunday Mr. Councilman will present the best 20 minutes you have ever heard on the book of Revelation. Read Rev. 1:19 and 22:18-19 before Sunday. It is not enough to read the Bible, it must be read correctly. God is knowable and makes Himself known. Jesus Christ is the scarlet thread throughout all Scripture. The goal of theology and Bible study is transformation, not just information.

Lesson 51 Year in Review

Postcard: Your parents have received a list of all the things we studied this year. You should be able to tell them a sentence or maybe a paragraph about every topic on the list. Maybe they will review with you as you prepare for the final exam on May 26 before you move up to the 7th grade! (Next class is May 26th.) Read Psalms 90:1-4.

Lesson 52 The Final Exam

Postcard: We conclude this 6th grade year in Sunday School with a final reminder of the importance of reading God's Word every day. Do you remember the three-part system we use for studying Scripture? 1--When the Bible can be taken literally, it should be taken literally. 2--It is a progressive unfolding of truth. 3--the New Testament prevails when it comments upon the Old Testament. The Holy Spirit enlarges our understanding of Scripture as we read it more, building truth upon truth. It's somewhat like climbing mountains. The higher you climb, the clearer the air and the farther you can see. Never stop climbing. Arrive Sunday eager to demonstrate on the Final Exam what you have learned this year. Read Psalm 100.

Lesson 53 Farewell

Postcard: Your year in the 6th grade boys Sunday School class has ended. If you have read the Word daily and followed the guidance from your weekly post cards, then you have built a basic understanding of the New Testament, and learned a system of study that will serve you well as you continue to study God's Word. Read Proverbs 3:5-6. When you see a covered bridge in the future, think of some Scriptural principles. The Bible presents a clearly defined pathway for your life, though the destination is not yet in view. The cover affords shelter, much like the comfort and assurance we find in Scripture. The bridge itself carries you safely across unseen trouble that awaits those who go another way. We will enjoy watching you grow spiritually as you learn more of the grace of God as you serve Him.

Lesson 54 Alumni Challenge

#Postcard: You have just completed one year studying the New Testament. You will now build upon that knowledge and use it to serve God for a lifetime. Former students have served the Lord as a surgeon, doctor, lawyer, dentist, soldier, college professor, pastor, military chaplain, businessman, salesman, banker, builder, graphic artist, and other roles. They have grown to be husbands, fathers, deacons, church officers, teachers and respected, faithful men. They have graduated from high school, of course, and Christian and secular colleges, earning bachelors, masters, and doctoral degrees, played sports at many levels, and placed their sons in the class you just completed. We urged you to use this time in your life to prepare for what God has ahead for you. What will you do with the talents God has given you? Will you join this long line of former Beacon Sixth Grade Boys who serve Him today in so many ways?

"Walt-isms"

When I wrote my first book, *"How to be the Salesman They Remember"* two pages at the end drew a lot of attention—20 quotes I had used, that others called "The Walt-isms." Here are a few:

Success in life is finding God's will for your life...and following it.

The mind, once expanded by a new idea, never returns to its former size.

The person who does not read is no better off than one who cannot read.

If there isn't time to do it right, when will there be time to do it twice?

Many today know the cost of everything and the value of nothing!

Whoever rides a tiger can never dismount.

Exceed expectations the first three times and folks will value working with you. Then continue to exceed their expectations.

Whatever you reward, you'll get more of and whatever you punish you'll get less of. (Need proof? Just observe a mother with a 2-year-old in the grocery store!)

You do not get what you expect, you get what you inspect.

Sometimes it's dangerous to pay too little!

Sometimes we make things look so easy, folks think anyone can do it.

Never carry anything that will roll.

Your work is a means or way of life, but it is not life itself.

I know you've heard this one elsewhere, but remember the 5 Ps: Prior Planning Prevents Poor Performance.

And two new ones:

The musician's motto: **Except one tooteth their own horn, by whom shall it be tooted?**

Walt's breakfast motto: **Don't muzzle the oxymoron who fries your bacon.**

A Grades 1-5 Resource

Nathan Johnson, **our former Sunday School student,** has created a curriculum for grades 1-5. Here's his story:

The Mission of BetterBibleTeachers.com

We are dedicated to teaching God's Word to kids in *crazy interesting* ways. I really love teaching God's Word to kids regularly in elementary grades 1-5 in Sunday School in my Baptist church in San Diego, CA.

Many kids in Sunday Schools today who should be listening to the lesson, instead are squirming in their seats or goofing off with the kids around them. At church we are presenting the most valuable information a kid could ever hear.

I'm doing something about this. I present the life-changing and unchanging truth of God's Word in ways kids 6-10 will enjoy—while really listening. His Word transforms lives. Presentation of God's Word should be interesting to kids.

With over 250 lessons, BetterBibleTeachers.com equips elementary teachers. Membership to his unique grades 1-5 curriculum is offered on a monthly or an annual basis.

You'll see Sunday School object lessons, 28 Bible Verses for Kids to Know by Heart, How To Explain Faith to Sunday School Kids, How to teach Sunday School, and How To Train Teachers. **THANK YOU, NATHAN (Class of 1995).**

Note: Walt's book is most applicable for 6th grade through adult classes—emphasizing Bible reading. Nathan's work is created for lower grades, particularly for the youngest students who have not yet advanced in reading.—WA

---

16 All Scripture is given by inspiration of God, and is profitable for doctrine, for reproof, for correction, for instruction in righteousness, 17 that the man of God may be complete, thoroughly equipped for every good work.—2 Timothy 3:16-17

A Way to Honor Students

Before you need a special gift or award consider developing a relationship with a reliable custom gift artist. We rely on a private source. Numerous sources have online catalogs, perhaps even including someone in your area.

Custom gifts for Christmas, graduation or a special occasion for a student or others can be very meaningful. Items come from an array of die-cut ornaments, large engraved wall plaques or small free-standing ones with artistic beveled edges. Wooden engraved desk nameplates are among many good ideas. Many favorite hymns, verses or quotations are impressive engraved on a large wooden plaque or printed on paper for framing. Hymns may include the score or just the words.

Here's what appeared on a desk nameplate we presented to

DR. NATHAN PHILLIPS

a former student when he earned his professional degree.

Three Suppliers in the Text

amazingmail.com for picture post cards
shutterfly.com for prints of your photos
hendricksonrose.com for pamphlets